IMPROVE

YOUR

BRAIN POWER

IN ONLY 10 DAYS

A STEP-BY-STEP GUIDE
TO KEEPING YOUR BRAIN YOUNG AND
IMPROVING YOUR MEMORY

STEVEN McRYAN

DISCLAIMER

All the material contained in this book is provided for educational and informational purposes only. No responsibility can be taken for any results or outcomes resulting from the use of this material. While every attempt has been made to provide information that is both accurate and effective, the author does not assume any responsibility for the accuracy or use/misuse of this information.

TABLE OF CONTENTS

CHAPTER 1 : INTRODUCTION 1

CHAPTER 2 : EXERCISE 11

CHAPTER 3 : HEALTHY NUTRITION......................22

CHAPTER 4 : SLEEPING.....................................38

CHAPTER 5 : READING.....................................42

CHAPTER 6 : POSITIVE THINKING....................54

CHAPTER 7 : LISTENING TO MUSIC 70

CHAPTER 8 : VISUALIZATION......................87

CHAPTER 9 : ELIMINATING STRESSORS...............96

CHAPTER 10 : HAVE A LAUGH 109

CHAPTER 11 : SMART DRUGS...........................124

CONCLUSION.....................................132

CHAPTER 1

INTRODUCTION

The human brain is a comprehensive group of cells and about fifty million neurons that labour with the greatest complexity to keep the body in good health. Thus, having a healthier brain will lead to having a healthier body.

A human brain is thought to be five times the size of other mammals with similar body size. In human beings, the forebrain and frontal lobes are particularly expanded because these parts are the ones in charge of self-discipline, planning and analysis.

It is through the early stages of our lifetime that the development of the brain and the central nervous system is crucial. As the body grows older, its ability to take in nutrients weakens, and so it becomes a lot harder for the body to ward off illnesses and stresses. At the same time, during the aging process, we also lose neurons, or what are usually known as brain cells.

Other body cells have the ability to regenerate, but neurons (brain cells) do not regenerate nor do they replicate. So, as we get older, the brain becomes poorer in neurons and is therefore not capable of functioning as well as it used to when it was younger. In order to keep this important organ

functioning at its bestwe have to put into action several strategies, while at the same time avoiding activities that have the potential to harm it. This way, we can assist our brain to preserve its fitness and strength.

Studies show that mental decline is not an inevitable part of ageing. Like anything else, using your brain will make it work best. After all, there must be some truth in the saying "use it or lose it". It's a question of keeping your mind in trim to retain your mental abilities. Keeping yourself mentally, as well as physically fit, will make you feel better, improve brain power and help you to stay independent for longer. They say that "you can't teach an old dog new tricks"; but when it comes to the brain, scientists have discovered that this old adage simply isn't true. The human brain has an astonishing ability to adapt and change even in old age. This ability is known as neuroplasticity. With the right stimulation, your brain can form new neural pathways, alter existing connections, and adapt and react in ever changing ways.

The brain's incredible ability to reshape itself holds true when it comes to learning and memory. You can harness the natural power of neuroplasticity to increase your cognitive abilities, enhance your ability to learn new information, and improve your memory.

There is no getting away from the fact that the human brain is an astonishing piece of kit, and whilst we actually use more of our brains than some people may have us believe, scientists are still a long way from discovering the full potential of it. Many of us experience days when even the

simplest of decisions can prove to be very hard work; alternatively, we may suddenly find ourselves losing theability to remember things. This can be frustrating, especially if you haven't yet reached an age where you can be forgiven for doing so.

If we want to keep our memories from deteriorating, we need to find a solution before we are even confronted with the actual problem. Most people start to experience memory loss as they get older. To avoid this, you want to do everything possible to keep that gray matter in your head healthy. Otherwise, you could very well experience memory loss. This can be very inconvenient and debilitating.

No one wants to have to resort to the use of drugs and medicine to remedy their illnesses. In fact, the use of natural remedies is to be preferred. Drugs carry with them all sorts of side effects. The best natural remedy for avoiding any illness is to prevent it from happening in the first place. Your memory is no different. Luckily, there are several natural ways to keep your brain strong.

Try and quit all medications if you are taking any. They could be affecting your memory. Of course, this may be difficult. For example, you just can't come off diabetes medication because you want to improve your memory. However, you could be off diabetes medication in a year. Building up to walking an hour a day and eating right could help you lose the weight necessary to come off your medication.

An Improved Brain Equals to An Improved Life

The brain is the center of our universe, it is our character, our personality. When the brain is working properly, we will be, too.

We hear that we use less than 20% of our brain. What a waste! Do we have any other organs that we use so little? I, somehow, doubt that we have so much excess that we only need to use 20% to be "normal". I would suggest that we do, in fact, use 100% of our brains. The creator is not that wasteful.

We are blessed with a Spiritual Mind, or Higher Self, which is frequently ignored and almost always misunderstood (hence the 20%). This Higher Self expresses our Innate Divine Nature. You can merge into the awareness and energies of the Higher Self by opening your Seven primary Chakras. Here, you are able to perceive all forms of ideas and knowledge within the proper perspective. This will bring you emotional healing and strength. You are a far more powerful being than you think you are. Your Higher Self is your connection to the universe. Thankfully, the Higher Self is not easily distorted by our Illusions; luckily, we can have clear intuitive insights and new truths. The Higher Self brings clarity to the abstract body, which in turn helps reveal our creativity and inner strength through concrete thinking. All with the aid of our mental body.

The Mental Body is concerned with knowledge and/or concrete thinking, while the Etheric Body is concerned with

Wisdom, which results from the many lifetime experiences. The Higher Self brings to us Insights which are clear and help us purify our perceptions of the truth.

The brain is truly amazing when it comes to all the memories, thinking and reasoning abilities that it encompasses, along with our creative capabilities that all allow us to relate meaningfully to our world. Biologists have come to the conclusion that genes are not the only influences in the intercellular game which have an impact on our personal health. The cell membrane, the part of the cell that senses and responds to the surrounding environment, the cells brain if you want, is profoundly important. What is it that talks to your cells and your organs, telling your heart to beat and your organs to function? It is a separate nerve system connected to your brain.

We have discovered that we can use brain wave vibration training to allow your brain stem to work as it was always meant to work. Life is supposed to be free and natural. Unfortunately, we often suppress the natural ability of the brain because of the stress and emotions that we fall prey to every day. You may be amazed to know that every living creature possesses natural healing abilities, which is essentially the power to bring one's body back a normal state of health. With the stress and problems we find ourselves dealing with in today's society, it is increasingly difficult, or even close to impossible, to get back to a normal state of health. Sadly, many in our society are turning to drugs and alcohol to find relief.

We need to get ourselves back on track and get in touch with the Higher Self. We need to open the seven Chakras so we can tap into the ideas and knowledge that we all have and deserve, with complete clarity. We must do this naturally, without the use of drugs and alcohol. Be very careful! We could easily get onto the road to disaster, and without help, we might continue along that road. Brain wave vibration training using Binaural Beats will definitely help us turn all of this around naturally. In many of the early writings, references to vibrations were often deleted. This led to a lack of information and brought us to where we are today.

Do you want to improve your memory? Then read on! This feat can be relatively easy to accomplish. We automatically expect our brains to perform a variety of functions at the same time. We expect our memory to kick into gear and provide us with names, phone numbers, and a host of information at a split second's notice. There are times when our memory fails us, though, and we want to know why.

Have you ever experienced that embarrassing moment when you forget someone's name even if you have just met? I bet you have! When we experience these embarrassing moments, we tend to blame it on a variety of reasons. How often have you blamed your failing memory on your age? However, you'll be happy to know that age is not always the problem. There are a variety of reasons for a short memory failure. Researchers have proven that the mind can continue to develop at any age.

Similar to the muscles in your body, your mind must receive daily exercise. Despite your age or physical condition, you can still begin to improve your memory.

So many times we blame ourselves for having a poor memory, when in fact the problem is that we just aren't paying attention. Our lives have become so complicated that we are constantly trying to multitask. So, when we start to forget the simple things, like where we placed our keys or a particular document, we blame it on our failing memories. The truth is, we were probably busy doing something else or paying attention to something else when we misplaced our keys or that document. Our memory is not to blame; we simply weren't paying attention in the first place.

Here is a simple memory technique you can use to remember someone's name when you're being introduced to them. During the introduction, repeat the person's name; for example: "It's very nice to meet you, John" or "I have been looking forward to meeting you, John." The few extra seconds it takes to prolong the introduction and repeat the person's name is usually all the time required to help retain this information. Another great habit to get into is to look a person in the eyes when you are shaking hands repeating their name, and try to remember their eye color. This simple practice will keep your mind engaged in the present moment.

Common Ways to Improve Your Memory

Most people suffering from memory problems are delighted to find out that the exercises required to keep our brain strong are things that most of us do on a daily basis anyway. People are usually waiting for some strange and secret technique to make the brain more powerful. You'll likely be waiting a long of time for that kind of technique. The key to keeping your brain super strong is right in front of you. Everything you need may very well be in your home as we speak.

Reading is one of the most powerful ways of improving a poor memory. More importantly, it's an equally powerful way to maintain the strength of an already strong brain. Reading is awesome exercise for the brain. So, by doing more of it, your brain cannot help but to increase in strength and power. Not only will you learn, but the new stuff will also strengthen your brain. Just the act of engaging your mind in the activity of reading is exercise enough.

Remedies for improving your memory are probably the most entertaining of all ailment treatments. If you're trying to get your heart in shape, you have to start exercising every day by running or walking. That can be boring. However, if you want to improve your memory, you can very simply start by playing card games every day. The ones on your computer will work just fine. One of my favorites is spider solitaire. It's a very addicting game. Using it to prove your memory will be the easiest medicine you've ever used to remedy an ailment.

Keep your doctor informed about any issues you may be experiencing with your memory. If you are dealing with memory loss, there could be a dead canary in the mine. Memory loss could be an indication of the onset of a serious illness, such as Alzheimer's. Just like exercising physically is a good way to prevent the onset of heart disease, so is keeping the brain healthy an effective way of preventing the onset of Alzheimer's. Start the brain-exercise regimen today!

It doesn't matter how brainy you are or how much education

you've had. You can still improve and expand your mind. Boosting your mental faculties doesn't have to mean studying hard or becoming a reclusive bookworm. There are lots of tricks, techniques and habits, as well as changes to your lifestyle, diet and behaviour that can help you flex your grey matter and get the best out of your brain cells.

In the following chapters, you'll find out about 10 daily habits that will provide you with step-by-step guidance on your journey towards improving your brain power in just 10 days. These include:

Exercise

Healthy Nutrition

1. Sleeping

2. Reading

3. Positive Thinking

4. Listening to Music

5. Visualization

6. Eliminating Stressors

7. Having a Laugh

8. Smart Drugs

Thinking of your brain as a muscle is actually a great analogy, even if it's not technically accurate. If you don't exercise a muscle, it weakens; it atrophies. If you exercise that muscle in exactly the same way over and over, day in and day out, the muscle won't atrophy, but it won't grow or develop either. If you consistently use that muscle in new ways, whether you stretch it, push it or challenge it, you'll help it grow and make it stronger. That's exactly the way the brain works. Challenge your brain in new ways as often as possible, and you'll be stronger and smarter than you were the day before.

CHAPTER 2

EXERCISE

Exercise helps memory and thinking through both direct and indirect means. The benefits of exercise come directly from its ability to reduce insulin resistance, reduce inflammation, and stimulate the release of growth factors (chemicals in the brain that affect the health of brain cells, the growth of new blood vessels in the brain, and even the abundance and survival of new brain cells).

Indirectly, exercise improves mood and sleep, and reduces stress and anxiety. Problems in these areas frequently cause or contribute to cognitive impairment.

Many studies have suggested that the parts of the brain that control thinking and memory (the prefrontal cortex and medial temporal cortex) have greater volume in people who exercise by comparison with people who don't. "Even more exciting is the finding that engaging in a program of regular exercise of moderate intensity over six months or a year is associated with an increase in the volume of selected brain regions," says Dr. Scott McGinnis, a neurologist at Brigham and Women's Hospital and an instructor in neurology at Harvard Medical School.

While you might know that you need to exercise your body, did you know that it might also be important to exercise your mind? You've probably heard the old adage "use it or lose it." Many researchers do believe that this maxim applies to your brain health.

Brain training is all the rage these days, often touted as a way to sharpen your mind and even boost intelligence. While many cognitive scientists suggest that the claims surrounding brain training are both exaggerated and misleading, there is an abundance of research suggesting that certain types of activities can be beneficial for your brain's health.

The brain's plasticity allows it to adapt and change, even as you grow older. As you learn new things, you can create and strengthen neural pathways and networks. This helps make your brain stronger, but it can also help make it more flexible and adaptable to change.

9 Exercises To Increase Your Brain Power

We all want to hit the gym at some point in our lives in an attempt to get the perfect beach body for the summer, or simply to tone our muscles and stay in shape. Building muscles might be our goal, but how often do we think about building our brain? Chances are that most people don't even realize what a great impact exercise has on their brain and how greatly it helps to boost brain power.

Working out appears to stimulate the hippocampus, the brain region associated with learning and memory. A recent study found that rats doing six to eight weeks of aerobic exercise had between two and three times more hippocampus neurons compared with rats that did no training. According to several studies and researches, a single exercise session can help enhance our cognitive abilities and improve mental focus better than a cup of coffee. A study conducted on teens and young adults also found that 10 to 40 minutes of exercise can give an immediate boost tobrain power and increase concentration levels by improving blood flow to the brain.

Hence, here are the top 9 exercises that can help increase your brain power and keep you mentally charged:

1. ***Squat your way through brain fatigue:*** While squats may seem like a very common or mainstream exercise, recent developments have come up with a very unusual twist to it. This upgraded version of squats has been found to improve mental health and has proved to be a very useful exercise when wishing to alleviate brain fog or any kind of mental dullness.

   To get started, you need to stand as you normally would when performing a squat, with your feet pointing straight and set apart at shoulder width. Then grab your right earlobe with your left hand's thumb and finger; Repeat the step for your left earlobe and right hand's fingers. Then lower down in a squat position while breathing in, and breathe out as you stand back up. Continue the movement for a couple of minutes or for as long as you can muster.

2. ***Clear your mind with a set of planks:*** Planks will not only give you a pair of perfectly toned legs and a full body workout, but will also help you with mental clarity. When you are holding a plank or lying down in a plank position, you need to exert all your focus

and energy on the move. Although this exercise does require you to use your brain power to execute it perfectly, it also helps relieve all the stress and thus clear the mind. In addition, planks can work as a great tool for meditation.

However, keep in mind that you need to perform this exercise properly in order to maximize its results. So, start by getting on the floor face down; use your toes and forearms to rise, keeping your body in a long straight line. Your back should be flat and your abs tucked in. While your legs should be extended behind you, your head and neck need to remain in a neutral position. Hold this position for a few seconds and repeat.

3. ***Jump those jacks to kick start your brain:*** Typically used as a warm-up exercise before starting tough workout regimes, jumping jacks are packed with brain-boosting power. They get your blood pumping hard and fast, and simultaneously improve its supply to the brain. This, in turn, gives your brain an energy boost which keeps it functioning without wearing out. If you perform this kind of activity for just ten minutes, your brain is sure to get a massive boost of power.

All you need in order to perform this exercise effectively is to stand tall with your hands by your side and feet positioned together. Now, simultaneously raise your arms above your head and jump, putting your feet to the sides; then bring both arms and feet back to the starting position. Keep moving back and forth between the jumping and standing position so that your body temperature goes up.

4. ***Run for your life:*** Running may come off as very simple, but its benefits are endless. Research conducted by a team of Australian scientists has concluded and confirmed that running isn't only great for the heart, but is also excellent for the brain and mind.

   The research also came up with evidence strong enough to prove that running enhances our cognitive function and helps the brain tremendously. This suggests that a program that includes aerobic exercises along with resistance-type training is excellent for both your body and your brain. So, try running for 30-40 minutes every day and observe great changes in how your brain functions.

5. ***Walking never gets old:*** If all else fails or seems hard to manage, walk. Walking is perhaps one of the most common and effective exercises, giving your body an all-rounder boost. From your brain to your toes, everything is impacted by a few minutes of regular walking.

   Research has it that adults who take a stroll a few times a week experience improvement in their brain power and have less of a risk of illnesses like Alzheimer's, which rob a person of their memory. According to the results of an exercise program that involved walking, those in the exercise group did better on cognitive tests and had sharper memories than those who didn't exercise at all.

6. ***A few breathing exercises go a long way:*** Who knew breathing had something to do with your brain power?! Yes, that's right! Breath-holding exercises in particular have shown great promise and led to significant progress in stressful situations. These exercises help a person exert control over things and allow them full command over their mental reserves. Holding your breath and then releasing it slowly pushes you into a state of flow where your brain activity gets significantly stimulated. The frequency of electrical impulses greatly increases, which ensures an energy rush to the brain.

   All you are required to do to perform these breathing exercises correctly is sit back and relax, inhale, hold it in for a while and then exhale. Repeat this for as long as you can or till your brain feels active and running again.

7. ***Yoga cleanses the soul and mind:*** Widely practiced worldwide for health benefits and relaxation, yoga is a spiritual and ascetic discipline that involves certain meditation procedures and exercise postures that target specific body parts. In fact, according to research, the practice of yoga helps boost memory and can also improve brain vitality. Yoga encompasses numerous exercise postures which are targeted towards specific areas, but the one with the

shoulder stand improves the supply of blood to the brain the most. This has a positive impact on the cells of the brain and helps enhance a person's memory while also providing it with energy. Another pose called the 'intense forwarding bending' is particularly beneficial for increasing brain power and sharpening the memory. It helps the blood rush to your brain, too, which also boosts the functions of this organ.

Hence, incorporating certain yoga poses in your everyday routine can significantly improve the way your brain functions and also relieves mental stress and anxiety.

8. ***Tai Chi "take a leaf out of the Chinese's books":*** Typically known as a gentle exercise that originated in China, Tai Chi has come to be known as a form of 'meditation in motion', which influences brain activity and works as a great stress reliever.

Numerous studies conducted to study the effect of Tai Chi on the brain have concluded that this type of exercise increases the size of the brain and enhances a person's memory and thinking, thus improving brain power.

Other studies show that a regular Tai chi exercise regimen improves cognitive abilities, especially in elderly people, and also enlarges the brain significantly.

9. ***Weight training coupled with resistance exercises:***

Last but not the least, lifting weights combined with vigorous resistance exercises that involve severe contractions show that these can greatly improve memory and reasoning in people, particularly those that have mild cognitive impairment.

A combination of weight and resistance training exercises also significantly boosts brain power in people over the age of 50, and evidently affects an individual's brain health. Systematic studies that were conducted to assess the influence of weight lifting exercises showed a highly positive impact on brain capacity, alertness, attention, and memory. Resistance training also brings about a distinct effect on executive functions and the working memory.

While numerous people resort to brain-boosting foods and supplements, for example various super foods, vega protein, and herbs, which also work really well for the brain, the exercises presented above are a sure shot towards giving energy to your brain and improving its function. So, make sure you include some of these exercises in your workout regime to enjoy maximum benefits.

The next time you're looking to boost your brain power in business, instead of pouring yourself another cup of coffee, go exercise instead. Turn exercise into a can't-live-without habit by stepping away from life for 30 minutes or so every day and doing something you enjoy. Put on your workout clothes, lace up your running (or dancing) shoes and get moving! Your body will be better for it, as will your brain.

Children Who Exercise Have More Brain Power

We know that exercise boosts memory and thinking skills. But now researchers have shown for the first time that physical activity can increase the size of children's brains and improve academic performance.

The study carried out by a team from the University of Granada, Spain found that children who are physically fit have a greater volume of grey matter in the brain's frontal and temporal regions and the calcarine cortex, all of which are important for executive function (the mental skills that help us get things done), as well as learning, motor skills and visual processing. The researchers aimed to determine whether the brains of physically fit children were different to those of their less-fit peers, and if this affected their academic performance.

"The answer is short and forceful: yes, physical fitness in children is linked in a direct way to important brain structure differences, and such differences are reflected in the children's academic performance," said lead researcher Francisco B Ortega, of the University of Granada's Sport and Health Institute.

The study, published in the NeuroImage journal, is part of the ActiveBrains project, a randomized clinical trial involving more than 100 overweight and obese children aged between 8 and 11. The researchers found that motor ability helped boost grey matter in two regions which are essential for language processing and reading: the inferior frontal gyrus and the superior temporal gyrus. However, they identified no link between muscular strength and the volume of grey matter in any part of the brain.

The main author of the paper, Irene Esteban-Cornejo, a post-doctoral researcher at the University of Granada, said that grey-matter volume in the cortical and sub-cortical regions influenced by physical fitness improved the children's academic performance. Moreover, she added: "Physical fitness is a factor that can be modified through physical exercise, and combining exercises that improve the aerobic capacity and the motor ability would be an effective approach to stimulate brain development and academic performance in overweight and obese children."

The number of overweight or obese children is on the rise around the world, increasing from 32 million globally in 1990 to 41 million in 2016. Obesity rates are also climbing far faster in developing countries than in high-income countries, as economic prosperity leads to changing diets and lifestyles. The researchers at the University of Granada have urged policy-makers and educators to put their findings into practice in schools by teaching physical education every day.

If there was a magic pill that you could take that would improve your memory, concentration, mood, self-esteem, well-being, ability to deal with stressful situations, cognitive functioning, and boost your energy, this pill would be the most popular drug on the market. Exercising helps you in all respects; basically, it is a free and guaranteed way to make you think and feel better. So, what are you waiting for?! Put down your phone, log off your computer, and go for a walk, play some sport or go to the gym. Your mind will thank you for it!

21

CHAPTER 3

HEALTHY NUTRITION

In order to increase brain power, proper nutrition guidelines should be followed. Almost every type of food has a different effect on the brain, and with the variety of foods out there, it can be difficult to differentiate between the ones that don't bring much and the ones that can actually assist you the most. Specific types of vitamins and foods, in general, can help with the retention of memory and focus, while other vitamins and foods help with the prevention of brain degradation. Learning about the many vitamins that can be beneficial for your brain can help improve your brain health for the long term.

Taking in the right vitamins is essential if your goal is to improve your brain power. Every vitamin has a specific effect on the brain, so understand each accordingly. Vitamins like B12, B6, Zinc, and fatty acids like Omega-6 and Omega-3 all have positive effects on memory retention, the ability to focus and overall brain nourishment. You can find these vitamins in many of the health foods available in grocery stores. The funny thing is that most would not expect some of these foods to contain nutritious ingredients meant specifically for the brain.

A few nutritional foods that can enhance the brain include

green vegetables, nuts and seeds. Nuts and grains contain a ton of fatty acids and the B6 vitamin, which will help increase concentration. These foods can reduce your risk of Alzheimer's and memory-loss diseases in general. The reduction of brain tissue with proper nutrition intake can easily be noted in elder individuals who still have retained their memory and cognitive functions.

Other helpful foods include fish and eggs, which contain many essential fatty acids that prevent memory loss and improve the function of the brain.

Believe it or not, chocolate is known to contain great nutritional value for the overall health of our brains. The antioxidants found in chocolate have been noted to increase brain health over time; however, that does not mean you should load up on chocolate daily. Eating chocolate in moderation can also improve the body's overall function.

Spicy foods are known to improve brain health. Curry, in particular, has been known to lower the risk of diabetes and heart disease. It can also help with the eradication of free radicals that may potentially destroy your cognitive ability. Free radicals can cause inflammation within the brain; thanks to the antioxidants present in curry, these free radicals can be eliminated.

Taking in the proper nutrition can significantly improve your health and increase brain power if used on a consistent basis. Although each type of vitamin performs a different function for the brain, using them all in conjunction can benefit you in the long run. Since the brain is the most essential part of the body, keeping it healthy will benefit the body in its entirety.

Boost Your Brain Power With The Right Nutrition

We've known for decades how our food and drink choices affect our heart, liver and other parts of our body. Now we're seeing that the same holds true for the brain.

Mounting research shows that a healthy diet improves brain performance and preserves brain function. It makes sense – we know diet choices affect blood sugar, blood pressure and cholesterol. When any of these levels are off, the imbalance can have repercussions on the brain and increase the risk of stroke, dementia and impaired cognition.

Many people ask if there's a specific diet or special foods they should eat for more brain power. It's hard to name exactly which kind of diet is best for the brain, but we now have some clues, with research being done on the Mediterranean, DASH (Dietary Approaches to Stop Hypertension) and MIND (Mediterranean-DASH Intervention for Neurodegenerative Delay) diets.

All of these diets have certain factors in common: healthy fats such as nuts and fatty fish, limited saturated fat such as butter and coconut oils, plenty of fruits and vegetables, high-fiber whole grains and legumes, and very low amounts of processed and sugary foods such as fast food, chips, pastries and sweet drinks.

Let's look at how various nutrients affect the brain:

1. ***Fats:*** Okay, no jokes about 'fat heads.' Did you know that up to 70 percent of our brain is made of fat? Fat is very important for proper brain function, but it needs to be the right kind of fat. We need to consume enough omega 3-fatty acids because these are the essential building blocks of our brain, and they're important for learning and memory. This is one reason why women's prenatal vitamins contain DHA (docosahexaenoic acid), a type of omega-3 that's also found in large amounts in fatty fish, such as salmon and sardines. Another type of omega-3 is present in plants such as ground flaxseeds, chia, and walnuts.

   The fat you want to avoid in large amounts is saturated fat, which can be found in foods such as butter, fatty meat, whole-fat dairy products, and coconut oil. We need some, that's for sure, but most Americans eat too much of it.

   The worst fats are partially hydrogenated fats like trans fats, which are still found in some foods. Also, try to avoid mono- and di-glycerides. These fats have replaced trans fats in commercial cake mixes, frostings and other foods. It's also best to avoid any food that's deep fried, because these fats oxidize over time and may damage our cells.

2. ***Proteins:*** Proteins are important building blocks for

the neurotransmitters that send messages throughout the brain. Most of the research so far points to fish, poultry, eggs and plant-based proteins such as legumes and nuts as the healthiest sources.

Eggs have gotten a bad rap for their cholesterol content, but the newest research shows that eggs are fine for most people. In fact, they are a rich source of choline, which is important for brain function and especially important during pregnancy. You can also find choline in peanuts, beans, cauliflower and spinach.

3. ***Carbohydrates:*** Carbohydrates are starches and sugars that supply most of the fuel to our body, including our brain. It's the type and quality of carbohydrates that make a big difference. Focus on complex carbs, meaning ones that are high in fiber in their natural form – think 100 percent whole grains, beans, fruits and vegetables. They're packed with vitamins, minerals and antioxidants. These nutrients not only fuel the brain, but they also also protect brain cells against damage from free radicals released from pollution, stress and just being alive. Complex carbs take longer to digest, so they provide a steadier source of brain fuel compared to simple carbs such as candy, cookies and sweetened drinks.

One other note about carbs: the healthier ones have lots of fiber. Fiber feeds the good gut bacteria, which also appears to play a role in brain function. There's a lot of new research about the gut-brain connection and how our microbiome affects our 'second brain' in the gastrointestinal tract.

Check Your Dietary Pattern

Getting brain-health benefits from a healthy diet is a lot like training for a marathon. One or two days of healthy eating won't make up for several weeks of bad choices. The benefits come over time, and it's never too late to start.

The thing to remember is that improving brain function isn't just about eating one or two so-called super foods. It's the whole package that matters. The most important thing to look at is your 'dietary pattern' – the majority of foods that you eat most of the time. Do you eat fast food four or five times a week? Do you eat fruits and vegetables at most meals? Do you cook at home, but rely on processed mixes for meals? These are some of the questions to ask yourself when assessing how you are currently eating and what you can change for optimal brain health.

15 Foods to Boost Brain Power and Improve Memory Naturally

We all lead busy lives. Whether it's your job, kids, or a surprise bill for the month, life pulls at you constantly. You want to lead a healthy holistic lifestyle, but instead, you find that you are living a hectic one.

Your brain is also continually at work. It regulates thousands of complex functions, usually without bothering the conscious you with the exact details. But when you rely on fast food rather than whole-food, plant-based nutrition, you sacrifice your brain's abilities. Simple daily tasks can turn into complicated, complex problems if you do not fuel your brain correctly. You know that how you eat can affect your weight, but do you know how foods also affect your mood, brain power, memory, concentration, and even your ability to handle stress?

Here are some brain foods that will pull you out of your rut and improve your concentration:

i.   Avocado

ii.   Coconut Oil

iii.   Beans and Legumes

iv.   Blueberries

v.   Broccoli

vi.   Chia

vii.   Dark Chocolate

viii.   Nuts

ix.   Quinoa

x.   Red Cabbage

xi.   Rosemary

xii.   Spinach

xiii.   Sunflower Seeds

xiv.   Tomatoes

xv.   Whole Grains

How Your Brain Converts Food to Power

Before we talk about how the brain receives energy from food, we need to understand the process of ATP (Adenosine Triphosphate). ATP is broken down through hydrolysis whenever cells need energy. Through this process, your cells transfer energy to other organisms in the body, like the brain.

Your brain is a powerful organic machine. It controls all thought, movement, and sensation at blistering speed. It stores an immense amount of data as images, text, and concepts, and regulates circadian rhythm, hormone balance, breathing, and blood flow.

Weighing only 2% of our total body weight but consuming more than 20% of our caloric intake, our brain performs such strenuous functions that it becomes the most energy-greedy organ in our body. Half of your body's energy goes toward the bioelectrical messages your brain sends to neurons throughout the body.

The brain is a picky eater, too. Your brain demands a constant supply of glucose and not much else to keep it running; neurons don't store this basic sugar like other cells. They are always hungry and rather needy.

We obtain glucose from the carbohydrates we eat, such as fruits, vegetables, and grains. The brain may run on sugars, but this doesn't mean you can eat junk food. Refined sugars, like table sugar or high fructose corn syrup, aren't good options, since overly high blood glucose levels, or sugar spikes, damage your cells and brain. These types of sugars can literally starve our hungry neurons.

Insulin is a hormone that encourages cells to absorb and store glucose. As glucose enters the bloodstream from digestion, the pancreas releases just the right amount of insulin to keep blood sugar under control. However, when you consume refined sugars, glucose levels rise too high and too fast for your body to control despite the release of insulin.

This damages your liver and kidneys as your body tries desperately to rid itself of the sudden influx of excess glucose. Loose glucose can bind with protein to form very reactive free radicals that do damage everywhere they go. The pancreas responds by releasing more insulin than it normally does, and cells throughout the body respond by pulling in glucose as fast as possible. The extreme increase of insulin pulls down the dangerous blood sugar levels, but often they fall too low if your body has been forced to react so drastically. You flood your system with the incorrect fuel, and it feels good, but then your body has to do something to get rid of the refined sugar. This is why and how you experience a crash shortly after that sugar rush.

Since your neurons can't store glucose like other cells, they starve during this crash. The brain is forced to rob glucose from nearby fluids, and then it becomes sluggish as it runs low. Our memory and focus suffer during these low points.

There are also other nutrients the brain uses, though not as fuel. Our brains are made up of 60% fat, and low levels of fats can contribute to depression, Alzheimer's, and dementia.

You do have to choose good, healthy fats like those found in seeds, nuts, algae, coconut, and avocados. These fats contain the essential omega-3 and omega-6 fatty acids that we require for health, along with nonessential fatty acids that are also beneficial.

Saturated fats should be used in moderation, but can still be part of a healthy diet. Coconut oil has shown some potential in raising good cholesterol levels, promoting weight loss, and combatting brain disorders and degeneration. Trans fats found in hydrogenated vegetable oils are the ones to cut down on or avoid altogether. These fats raise cholesterol, damage the heart and the brain, and contribute to heart disease, obesity, and diabetes. Focus instead on adding good plant-based foods that boost brain function, mood, and memory.

Keep in mind that without good bacteria in our gut, our body has a difficult time absorbing nutrients from the food we consume, even if it is healthy. Probiotics are live bacteria that help our digestion and can even prevent or treat illnesses. Sunwarrior's probiotic capsules are vegan, aren't synthetic, and they contain prebiotics food for the good bacteria to thrive on.

Now, are you ready to take charge of your own health and improve your memory and concentration naturally, through food? Read on!

15 Foods to Boost Your Brain Power

1. *Avocado:* If avocado toast is one of your favorite breakfasts, then you are in luck. Avocados are a source of monounsaturated fats, omega-3, and

omega-6 fatty acids. These increase blood flow to the brain, lower cholesterol, and aid in the absorption of antioxidants.

Avocados also come with many antioxidants of their own, including vitamin E, which protect the body and the brain from free-radical damage. They are also a good source of potassium and vitamin K; both protect the brain from the risk of stroke.

You can include avocados into your diet by making guacamole, topping your power bowl with slices of it, or simply sprinkling some sea salt on it and eating it straight from the peel with a spoon.

2. ***Coconut Oil:*** Coconut oil has been called a superfood. Even if you don't use it to cook with, I'm sure you've seen the countless articles about the hundreds of beneficial ways to add it into your life.

   Coconut oil lives up to its claim to fame. It contains medium-chain triglycerides that the body uses for energy, leaving glucose for the brain. It also seems to have a beneficial effect on blood sugar, blood pressure, and cholesterol. Coconut oil acts as an anti-inflammatory and has been linked to helping prevent Alzheimer's and dementia.

3. ***Beans and Legumes:*** Though these may not be everyone's favorite food, beans and legumes are excellent sources of complex carbohydrates. They are also mixed with fiber, which slows absorption, providing our brains with a steady supply of glucose

without the risks of a sugar rush.

Beans and legumes are also rich in folate, a B vitamin critical for brain function, and essential omega fatty acids.

4. ***Blueberries:*** Blueberries are another superfood that is easy to incorporate into your diet. Protecting the brain from oxidative damage and stress, both of which lead to premature aging, Alzheimer's, and dementia, these berries are antioxidant powerhouses.
The flavonoids in blueberries also improve the communication between neurons. This effect increases memory, learning, reasoning, decision making, verbal comprehension, and all cognitive functions. Other dark berries such as blackberry, açai, and goji berries are good for the brain, too.

5. ***Broccoli:*** You may love broccoli, or you may hate it. The fact remains that the nutrients within broccoli are vital for your brain. This vegetable is rich in calcium, vitamin C, B vitamins, beta-carotene, iron, fiber, and vitamin K. These nutrients protect against free radicals, keep the blood flowing well, and remove heavy metals that can damage the brain.

    In addition to what broccoli does for your brain, it also has other amazing health benefits for your body. Broccoli is so great that we wrote an entire article on all that it has to offer.

6. ***Chia:*** Chia seeds are rich in omega 3 fatty acids and

both soluble and insoluble fiber. These powerful little seeds help control blood glucose levels, are anti-inflammatory, aid in hydration, and also contain many antioxidants.

The easiest and fastest way to incorporate these into your diet is to sprinkle them on top of a smoothie bowl or yogurt.

7. **Dark Chocolate:** You love chocolate and maybe even crave it right before you go to sleep at night. But did you know that the flavonols in chocolate improve blood-vessel function, which in turn improves cognitive function and memory? Chocolate also improves mood, eases pain, and is full of antioxidants.

To make the yummy bars in the photo, take a look at our recipe for these Raw Vegan Nanaimo Bars.

8. **Nuts:** Nuts are great in trail mix or alone as a snack. Walnuts and almonds are extremely good for the brain and nervous system. They are great sources of omega-3 and omega-6 fatty acids, vitamin B6, and vitamin E. Vitamin E has been shown to prevent many forms of dementia, and it improves brain power.

Nuts contain some anti-nutrients, like phytic acid. Since we consume a relatively small amount of nuts, this isn't a huge problem, but they are far healthier if you soak them overnight (about 8 hours) before eating them.

9. ***Quinoa:*** Like beans, legumes, and whole grains, quinoa is an excellent source of complex carbohydrates and fiber to balance blood sugar while providing the essential glucose the brain craves. Quinoa is also a good source of iron, which keeps the blood oxygenated, and B vitamins that balance mood and protect blood vessels.

   It is also gluten-free, for those who suffer from an allergy to this protein. And, like most seeds, grains, and nuts, quinoa contains phytic acid. In addition, it contains saponins, so it should be soaked overnight before being cooked.

10. ***Red Cabbage:*** Red cabbage is full of polyphenols, a powerful antioxidant that benefits the brain and the heart. Red cabbage also has glucosinolates compounds that fight cancer, decrease arthritis, and strengthen your bones to keep you young.

    Red cabbage is great in Asian-inspired meals and easily adds color to your plate. Part of maintaining a healthy diet is making sure you eat a variety of fruits and vegetables of different colors.

11. ***Rosemary:*** Rosemary has been shown to improve memory and cognitive function with its scent alone. It improves blood flow to the brain, balances your mood, and acts as an antioxidant. Rosemary is also a powerful detoxifier, fights cancer, boosts energy, and combats the aging of the skin.

    Rosemary is perfect for fall and holiday flavors.

12. ***Spinach:*** Spinach can prevent or delay dementia. The nutrients in spinach prevent damage to DNA, cancer cell growth, and tumor growth, but also slow the effects of aging on the brain. Spinach is also a good source of folate and vitamin E.

    If you hate the taste of raw or cooked spinach, don't worry. When you blend spinach in a smoothie, you can't taste it, but you still get all the amazing benefits.

13. ***Sunflower Seeds:*** Sunflower seeds and other seeds, like pumpkin, contain a rich mix of protein, omega fatty acids, and B vitamins. These seeds also contain tryptophan, which the brain converts into serotonin to boost mood and combat depression. The sprouts and microgreens of these seeds are even healthier.

    Seeds are great to eat by themselves, but you can also add them to your meal and side dishes.

14. ***Tomatoes:*** Tomatoes contain lycopene, a very powerful antioxidant that combats dementia and may improve mood balance, too. People suffering from Alzheimer's have lower levels of lycopene, so eating more tomatoes is essential for your health.

    When tomatoes are cooked, they transform into a 'cis-lycopene' form, which helps your body better absorb the tomato's nutrients.

15. ***Whole Grains:*** Carbs often are considered the enemy when it comes to healthy eating, but whole grains are rich in complex carbohydrates, fiber, and some

omega-3 fatty acids that shield the heart and brain from damaging sugar spikes, cholesterol, blood clots, and more. Grains also contain B vitamins that have a positive effect on your mood and the blood flow to the brain. Whole grains should be soaked, fermented, sprouted, or grown as microgreens to unlock all their nutritional power and minimize any anti-nutrients.

CHAPTER 4

SLEEPING

Never underestimate the power of a good night's rest. SKIMPING on sleep does awful things to your brain. Planning, problem-solving, learning, concentration, working memory and alertness all take a hit. IQ scores tumble. "If you have been awake for 21 hours straight, your abilities are equivalent to someone who is legally drunk," says Sean Drummond from the University of California, San Diego. And you don't even need to pull an all-nighter to suffer the effects: two or three late nights and early mornings on the trot have the same effect.

Luckily, the issue is reversible. If you let someone who isn't sleep-deprived have an extra hour or two of shut-eye, they perform much better than normally on tasks requiring sustained attention, such as taking an exam. And being able to concentrate harder has knock-on benefits for overall mental performance. "Attention is the base of a mental pyramid," says Drummond. "If you boost that, you can't help boosting everything above it."

These are not the only benefits of a decent night's sleep. Sleep is when your brain processes new memories, practises and hones new skills, and even solves problems. Say you're trying to master a new video game. Instead of grinding away into the small hours, you would be better off playing for a couple of hours, then going to bed. While you are asleep, your brain will reactivate the circuits it was using as you learned the game, rehearse them, and then shunt the new memories into long-term storage. When you wake up, hey, presto! You will be a better player. The same applies to other skills such as playing the piano, driving a car and, some researchers claim, memorising facts and figures. Even taking a nap after training can help, says Carlyle Smith of Trent University in Peterborough, Ontario.

There is also some evidence that sleep can help produce moments of problem-solving insight. The famous story about the Russian chemist Dmitri Mendeleev suddenly "getting" the periodic table in a dream after a day spent struggling with the problem is probably true. It seems that sleep somehow allows the brain to juggle new memories and thus produce flashes of creative insight. So, if you want to have your very own eureka moment, stop racking your brains and get your head down.

This can be another tricky area for entrepreneurs. Early mornings and late nights sometimes come with the territory, and the stresses or excitement that come with building and growing a business can have undesirable effects on sleep patterns. Sleep is required to consolidate memory and learning, though. If you don't get enough sleep, the gray-matter volume in your frontal lobe may begin to decrease. Your frontal lobe supports and controls your working memory as well as executive function, which makes it particularly important.

When you're sleep-deprived, your brain can't operate at full capacity. Creativity, problem- solving abilities and critical-thinking skills are compromised. But sleep is critical to learning and memory in an even more fundamental way. Research shows that sleep is necessary for memory consolidation, with the key memory-enhancing activity occurring during the deepest stages of sleep.

Many adults complain of sleep problems as they age, including insomnia, daytime sleepiness,and frequent waking during the night. But getting older doesn't automatically bring sleep problems. Poor sleeping habits are often the main causes of low–quality sleep in adults over 50.

- Sleep naturally boosts your melatonin levels at night.

- Artificial lights at night can suppress your body's production of melatonin, the hormone that makes you sleepy. Use low-wattage bulbs where safe to do so, and turn off the TV and computer at least one hour before bed.

- Make sure your bedroom is quiet, dark, and cool, and your bed is comfortable. Noise, light, and heat can interfere with sleep. Try using an eye mask to help block out light.

Turn off any electronics at least 30 minutes before going to bed. That means cell phones, computer, iPod, etc. Otherwise your brain will be over-stimulated as you're trying to sleep and you'll have greater difficulty in falling asleep and getting to the necessary stages of sleep.

For adults, it is best to get at least 8 hours of sleep every night.

- Develop bedtime rituals. A soothing ritual, like taking a bath or playing music, will help you wind down.

- Go to bed earlier. Adjust your bedtime to match the moments when you feel tired, even if that's earlier than it used to be.

Sleep is the magic pill. Your brain cannot function properly without a certain amount of sleep. Sleeping between 9pm and midnight ensures the best quality of sleep. It regenerates your cells and resets the mind for the next day's activities. When you sleep, you also process the information you learned the previous day, so you need as much sleep as possible in order to wake up with a clean slate and thus experience less stress and anxiety. If this is of concern to you, please consult your GP.

CHAPTER 5

READING

What books have you read lately? Reading relieves tension and stress. It also offers new information, which plays on your curiosity and expands the mind. The best part about reading is that it trains your mind to use your imagination, as it basically forces your brain to imagine what you are reading. Moreover, it improves your creativity while stimulating and adapting to new ideas and knowledge. The more you read, the more you can visualize using your imagination, the more you learn something new.

Learning something new gives your brain a workout in the same way that you would do a physical workout to increase your strength and endurance. If you stick to the well-worn paths of the stuff you already know, your brain isn't going to keep developing and growing.

Learning a language stimulates lots of different parts of your brain and helps make new neuro pathways. It takes plenty of mental effort and will help expand your knowledge base.

You could take up cooking, or knitting, or learning an instrument, or juggling. As long as you're enjoying yourself and learning new things, your brain will be happier and function better!

Enjoyment is an important part of learning and maintaining your brain's health and boosting its power. If you like what you're doing, there is more likelihood that you'll continue to be engaged and to learn.

Grab a Book

It seems there is wisdom to the old expression "Reading is fundamental," but in this case, the activity is also good for the mind. Thanks to the focus and relaxed state that is created when sitting down with a good book, reading can lower the blood pressure better than traditional methods, like drinking a glass of tea or chilling out to a mellow tune. A growing body of research suggests that it also helps in the development of the three types of intelligence: fluid, crystallized and emotional. Be sure to always pack a book in your bag for those sluggish moments in between daily activities.

Since reading is a form of escapism, it relieves tension and stress, which are brain-cell killers. In addition, research has shown that using your imagination is a great way to train your brain because you force your mind to "picture" what you are imagining. Reading is a great way to trigger your imagination!

Why You Should Read Every Day

When was the last time you read a book or a substantial magazine article? Do your daily reading habits center around tweets, Facebook updates, or the instructions on your instant oatmeal packet?

Since you were a child, you've probably been told to read because "it's good for you." Parents and doctors, teachers and librarians, even me on this very site have touted the many health and wellness benefits of books; but has anyone ever explained to you what reading actually does to your brain? You might be surprised to find out exactly what happens in your head when you crack open a book.

Reading is perhaps one of the best hobbies in the world, and one of the healthiest. Whether you're reading fiction or nonfiction, a newspaper or a poem, reading is not only educational and informative, it's entertaining and relaxing, too. And, although it is still a widely unexplored area, research on reading has already brought the many benefits of this activity to light.

Over the years, doctors, scientists, and researchers have confirmed that reading is a stress- reducing activity that can lower your heart rate and blood pressure. It's been proven to improve people's memories, increase brain power, and even enhance empathic skills. Reading has even been linked to longer life spans.

So, how exactly does reading do all that? Like so many other human phenomenons, it all starts with the brain. It may not feel like it, but when we are looking at words on the page, our brain is running several simultaneous processes, from word analysis and auditory detection to vocalization and visualization, to the experience we know and love called 'reading'.

If you're one of countless people who don't make a habit of

reading regularly, you might be missing out. Keep that in mind the next time you need an activity to kill your time and boost your brain power!

Reading has a significant number of benefits. Here are 10 that will get you to start reading.

1. ***Mental Stimulation:*** Studies have shown that staying mentally stimulated can slow the progress of (or possibly even prevent) Alzheimer's and Dementia, since keeping your brain active and engaged prevents it from losing power. Just like any other muscle in the body, the brain requires exercise to remain strong and healthy, so the phrase "use it or lose it" is particularly apt when it comes to your mind. Doing puzzles and playing games such as chess have also been found to be helpful when it comes to cognitive stimulation.

2. ***Stress Reduction:*** No matter how much stress you have at work, in your personal relationships, or countless other issues that you juggle with in your daily life, it all just slips away when you lose yourself in a great story. A well-written novel can transport you to other realms, while an engaging article will distract you and keep you in the present moment, letting tensions drain away and allowing you to relax.

3. ***Knowledge:*** Everything you read fills your head with new bits of information, and you never know when this information might come in handy. The more knowledge you have, the better equipped you are to

tackle any challenge you'll ever face.

Additionally, here's a bit of food for thought: should you ever find yourself in dire circumstances, remember that although you might lose everything else— your job, your possessions, your money, even your health— knowledge can never be taken from you.

4. ***Vocabulary Expansion:*** This goes hand in hand with the above topic: the more you read, the more words you gain exposure to. In the end, these will inevitably make their way into your everyday vocabulary.

   Being articulate and well-spoken is of great help in any profession, and knowing that you can speak to higher-ups with self-confidence can be an enormous boost to your self- esteem. It could even aid in your career, as those who are well-read, well-spoken, and knowledgeable on a variety of topics tend to get promotions more quickly (and more often) than those with smaller vocabularies and lack of awareness towards literature, scientific breakthroughs, and global events.

   Reading books is also vital for learning new languages, as non-native speakers gain exposure to words used in context, which will ameliorate their own speaking and writing fluency.

5. ***Memory Improvement:*** When you read a book, you have to remember an assortment of characters, their backgrounds, ambitions, history, and nuances, as

well as the various arcs and sub-plots that weave their way through every story. That's a fair bit to remember, but brains are marvellous things and can remember these things with relative ease.

Amazingly enough, every new memory you create forges new synapses (brain pathways) and strengthens existing ones, which assists in short-term memory recall as well as stabilizing moods. How cool is that?

6. ***Stronger Analytical Thinking Skills:*** Have you ever read an amazing mystery novel, and solved the mystery yourself before finishing the book? If so, you were able to put critical and analytical thinking to work by taking note of all the details provided and sorting them out to determine "whodunnit".

   That same ability to analyze details also comes in handy when it comes to critiquing the plot; determining whether it was a well-written piece, if the characters were properly developed, if the storyline ran smoothly, etc. Should you ever have an opportunity to discuss the book with others, you'll be able to state your opinions clearly, as you've taken the time to really consider all the aspects involved.

7. ***Improved Focus and Concentration:*** In our internet-crazed world, attention is drawn in a million different directions at once as we multi-task through everyday life.

   In a single 5-minute span, the average person will

divide their time between working on a task, checking email, chatting with a couple of people (via gchat, skype, etc.), keeping an eye on Twitter, monitoring their smartphone, and interacting with co-workers. This type of ADD-like behaviour causes stress levels to rise and lowers our productivity.

When you read a book, all of your attention is focused on the story; the rest of the world just falls away, and you can immerse yourself in every fine detail you're absorbing.

Try reading for 15-20 minutes before work (i.e. on your morning commute, if you take public transit), and you'll be surprised at how much more focused you are once you get to the office.

8. ***Better Writing Skills:*** This goes hand in hand with the expansion of your vocabulary; exposure to published, well-written work has a notable effect on one's own writing, as observing the cadence, fluidity, and writing styles of other authors will invariably influence your own work.

    In the same way that musicians influence one another and painters use techniques established by previous masters, so do writers learn how to craft prose by reading the works of others.

9. ***Tranquility:*** In addition to the relaxation that accompanies reading a good book, it's possible that the subject you read about can bring about immense inner peace and tranquility.

Reading spiritual texts can lower blood pressure and bring about an immense sense of calm, while reading self-help books has been shown to help people suffering from certain mood disorders and mild mental illnesses.

10. ***Free Entertainment:*** Though many of us like to buy books so we can annotate them and dog-ear pages for future reference, they can be quite pricey.

For low-budget entertainment, you can visit your local library and bask in the glory of the countless tomes available there for free. Libraries have books on every subject imaginable, and since they rotate their stock and constantly get new books, you'll never run out of reading material.

If you happen to live in an area that doesn't have a local library, or if you're mobility- impaired and can't get to one easily, you should know that most libraries have their books available in PDF or ePub format as well, so you can read them on your e-reader, iPad, or computer screen.

There are also many online sources where you can download free e-books, so go hunting for something new to read!

There's a reading genre for every literate person on the planet, and whether your tastes lie in classical literature, poetry, fashion magazines, biographies, religious texts, young adult books, self-help guides, street lit, or romance novels, there's something out there that will definitely capture your curiosity and imagination.

Step away from your computer for a little while, crack open a book, and replenish your soul for a little while. You will not regret it.

Why Reading Is The Best Workout For Your Brain

From relieving stress to improving brain function to increasing empathy, books are capable of doing a lot more than just entertaining the people who enjoy them. In fact, reading is the best workout for your brain, and it can even improve your memory. Sure, unwinding with Netflix at the end of every day is relaxing and all, but regularly reading is good for your mind, body, and soul.

We regularly obsess over the best ways to exercise our bodies: how to trim them or strengthen them, what to feed them or what to keep away from them. But how often do we think about exercising our brains? The most complex organ and command center of the whole body, the small, internal three-pound biological structure is responsible for so many important functions, yet it tends to get ignored, even taken for granted.

That is, until something goes wrong. Once this magical piece of machinery starts to break down, we start to worry about it, but what if instead of trying to treat a problem after it starts, we focused on preventative care and overall brain wellness? What if we exercised our brains like we do our bodies?

There are a lot of different ways you can treat your brain with love and care for its health that don't require a doctor's appointment, a prescription, or a trip to the gym. Plenty of foods, including salmon, nuts, and avocados, have been dubbed "brain foods" for their high omega-3 fats content, and doctors have long praised their effects on brain function and memory. Purveyors of sudoku and Sunday morning crossword-lovers have long believed in the power of puzzles to keep brains healthy and functioning at their highest levels.

According to scientists, though, one of the best ways you can exercise your brain is reading, and the reason why is all connected to memory. One of the brain's most important functions is memory. It is the storage center of everything a person has learned, including not only their own name and identity, and the identities of the people around them, but also the skills they need to function in everyday life. Without it, people struggle to make it through day-to-day life, as evident in the heartbreaking case of Alzheimer's disease, an illness 500,000 people die from every year. That's why it's crucial to continually work to engage the mind and improve memory.

Luckily, to do that, all you have to do is pick up a book. According to a study conducted at the Fisher Center for Alzheimer's Research Foundation, mental stimulation like reading can help protect memory and thinking skills, especially as people grow older. The authors of the study even suggest that reading every day can slow down late-life cognitive decline, keeping brains healthier and more functional for longer.

Ongoing studies and observations at Northcentral University led to similar findings. According to the graduate school's director, Dr. Wade Fish, reading has actually been shown to ensure a slower rate of memory deterioration and prevent the decline of other key mental capacities. This delayed decline means that older adults can stay mentally healthier for longer, which actually means reading can help people live longer.

The act of reading does a number of things that helps heighten overall brain function and increase memory. Scientists at the University of California, Berkeley, found that this activitycan lower the levels of beta-amyloid, a brain protein involved in Alzheimer's, by keeping the mind cognitively stimulated. Reading has also been linked to slowing mental decline by keeping important parts of the brain working, and improving overall mental flexibility, an important component to developing and retaining memory.

You may not be able to see it, but your brain is one of the most important parts of yourself. Without it and the memories it keeps, you wouldn't be you, let alone remember all of your favorite books. Luckily, just by reading them, you can help improve your memory and exercise your brain in the most fun and effective way.

Read Books That Push Your Boundaries

It's okay to take small steps on this one, but reading is one of the best things you can do for your brain. Maybe you just commit to turning off the TV (which is much more passive than reading) and instead picking up a book, any book, once in a while. Perhaps you branch out from your usual style of book. The point is to read something that's different from your usual fare, because if you broaden your reading horizons you're sure to get smarter. Swap your usual sci-fi for history occasionally, or trade your fluff for a classic from time to time. The point is to get out of your reading rut.

CHAPTER 6

POSITIVE THINKING

It's been said that, on average, humans can have anywhere from 12,000 to 60,000 thoughts per day, if not more. Positive thinking doesn't mean that you keep your head in the sand and ignore life's less pleasant situations. Positive thinking simply means that you approach unpleasantness in a more positive and productive way. You think the best is going to happen, not the worst.

Positive thinking often starts with self-talk. Self-talk is the endless stream of unspoken thoughts that run through your head. These automatic thoughts can be positive or negative. Some of your self-talk comes from logic and reason. Other self-talk may arise from misconceptions that you create because of lack of information.

If the thoughts that run through your head are mostly negative, your outlook on life is more likely pessimistic. If your thoughts are mostly positive, you're likely an optimist, someone who practices positive thinking.

The Health Benefits of Positive Thinking

Researchers continue to explore the effects of positive thinking and optimism on health. Health benefits that positive thinking may provide include:

a.   Increased life span

b.   Lower rates of depression

c.   Lower levels of distress

d.   Greater resistance to the common cold

e.   Better psychological and physical well-being

f.   Better cardiovascular health and reduced risk of death from cardiovascular disease

g.   Better coping skills during hardships and times of stress

It's unclear why people who engage in positive thinking experience these positive effects; one theory is that having a positive outlook enables you to cope better with stressful situations, which reduces the harmful health effects of stress on your body.

It's also thought that positive and optimistic people tend to live healthier lifestyles — they get more physical activity, follow a healthier diet, and don't smoke or drink alcohol in excess.

Focusing on Positive Thinking

You can learn to turn negative thinking into positive thinking. The process is simple, but it does take time and practice. You're creating a new habit, after all. Here are some ways to think and behave in a more positive and optimistic way:

a.   ***Identify areas to change:*** If you want to become more optimistic and engage in more positive thinking, first identify areas of your life that you usually think negatively about, whether it's work, your daily commute or a relationship. You can start small by focusing on one area that you believe you should approach in a more positive way.

b. ***Check yourself:*** Periodically during the day, stop and evaluate what you're thinking. If you find that your thoughts are mainly negative, try to find a way to put a positive spin to them.

c. ***Be open to humor:*** Give yourself permission to smile or laugh, especially during difficult times. Seek humor in everyday happenings. When you can laugh at life, you feel less stressed.

d. ***Follow a healthy lifestyle:*** Aim to exercise for about 30 minutes on most days of the week. You can also break your workout up into 10-minute chunks during the day. Exercise can positively affect mood and reduce stress. Follow a healthy diet to fuel your mind and body. Don't forget to learn techniques to manage stress.

e. ***Surround yourself with positive people:*** Make sure those in your life are positive, supportive people you can depend on to give helpful advice and feedback. Negative people may increase your stress level and make you doubt your ability to manage stress in healthy ways.

f. ***Practice positive self-talk:*** Start by following one simple rule: don't say anything to yourself that you wouldn't say to anyone else. Be gentle and encouraging with yourself. If a negative thought enters your mind, evaluate it rationally and respond with affirmations of what is good about you. Think about things you're thankful for in your life.

Eliminating Errors in Thinking

It is important to be aware of the psychological side of thinking. Brain prowess aside, we all make thinking errors. There are five different errors that psychologists have identified: Partialism, Adversary Thinking, Time Scale Error, Initial Judgment and arrogance and Conceit.

× *Partialism:* Errors that occur when the individual observes the problem through one's perspective only. That is, an individual examines only one factor of the problem, and most often than not arrives – quite naturally – at a premature solution.

× *Adversary Thinking:* This is the "you are the one who is wrong and thus I should be right" type of thinking. Politicians are the masters of this type of thinking and they use it to their advantage.

× *Time Scale Error:* This is a kind of partialism in thinking where the individual sees the problem from a limited time-frame. It can be likened to short-sightedness.

Initial Judgment - Here, the individual becomes very subjective. Instead of considering the issue or problem objectively, the individual approaches it with prejudice or bias.

Arrogance and Conceit - may also be referred to as the

"Village Venus Effect" because, like country people who think that the hottest girl in their village is the hottest girl in the world, the thinker believes that there is no better solution other than the one he has already found. This blocks creativity.

11 Ways to Boost Positive Thinking

When you harness the power of positivity, it's amazing how much of an impact this has on your life. It makes every moment worth experiencing and every goal worth shooting for. By thinking positive, you just can't help but be optimistic, even when everyone around you is miserable. As a result, you are happier, less depressed, and more satisfied.

The benefits of positive thinking are vast. So, how do you train your brain to think positive?

1. ***Ask yourself, "Do I think positively?"*** *:* Not sure whether you're a negative nelly? Take this well-being quiz, which not only gives you a score on "positivity," but also helps you identify the other skills that can contribute to your improving your happiness and well-being. If you're someone who needs to work on positivity, keep reading.

2. ***Strengthen your memory for positive information:*** Did you know that you may be able to increase your positivity just by memorizing lists of positive words? It's because when you force your brain to use positive words frequently, you make these words (and their basic meaning) more accessible, more connected, and more easily activated in your brain. So, when

you go to retrieve a word or idea from your memory, positive ones can come to the top more easily.

Not sure which words are positive? Psychologists have painstakingly measured thousands of words to determine how positive and negative they are. I've compiled only the most positive of the positive words into a positive word workbook for adults, and a positive word workbook for kids. If you're struggling to think positive, try this strategy first. It can help develop your brain in ways that may make the other positive-thinking strategies easier to implement.

3. ***Strengthen your brain's ability to work with positive information:*** Once your brain has built strong neural networks for positive words, try to extend these networks by asking your brain to use positive information in new ways. For example, you could memorize positive words and set an alarm that reminds you to recall these words, in reverse order, an hour later.

    Or you could print out these words on cards, cut them into two pieces, shuffle them all together and then find each card's match. For example, the word "laughter" would be cut into "laug" and "hter." To match the word pieces, your brain has to search through lots of positive information to find what it's looking for. This positive-memory-recall task may make it easier for you to think positive.

4. ***Strengthen your brain's ability to pay attention to the positive:*** Are you one of those people who notice

the bad stuff first, like when someone cuts you off in traffic or your food doesn't taste quite as good as you had wanted it to? Then you likely have trained your brain to focus on the negative, and your brain has gotten really good at it. It can be really challenging to undo this training. So instead, train your brain to be even better at focusing on the positive.

Just routinely focus on positive information and direct your attention away from the negative.

5. ***Condition yourself to experience random moments of positivity:*** Did you know that you can condition yourself for positivity? If you've ever taken an intro to a psychology course, you've probably heard about the study of Pavlov's dog. Here is a quick refresher:

Pavlov had a dog. Pavlov would ring a bell to tell his dog that it was almost feeding time. Like most dogs, Pavlov's dog would get really excited when he was about to get fed. So he'd drool all over the place. What happened? Well, suddenly Pavlov's dog started getting excited just by the sound of that bell, even when food wasn't present. Eating food and the sound of the bell became linked in the dog's brain. Something as meaningless as a bell was now making the dog excited.

This effect is called classical conditioning. The idea is that when two stimuli are repeatedly paired, the response that was first elicited by the second stimulus (food) is now elicited by the first stimulus alone (the bell). This happens all the time without us even realizing it. For example, the favorite food for many of us is something that we ate as a child with our families. What likely happened was that the positive feelings of being with family and the particular food got paired in our brains. As a result, we now get the warm- fuzzy feelings that we got from spending time with family just from eating the food alone, even if our family is not currently present when we eat it.

Although your environment conditions you to react in particular ways all the time, if you know what you're doing, you can use classical conditioning to boost your positivity. You do exactly what Pavlov did. You just repeatedly link boring things (like a bell ringing) with positive thoughts and feelings over and over again. Pretty soon, these boring things will generate positivity automatically. That's classical conditioning at work. This can help you think positively because when you are going about your life, maybe even feeling bummed about stresses or challenges, you'll have these little positive moments that keep you energized and in a good mood.

6. ***Think positive, but not too much, and think negative when you need to:*** Of course, thinking positive has its benefits. But thinking positive isn't always the best response. Negative thoughts sometimes have benefits, too.

When we are sad or grieving, thinking negative thoughts and showing the emotions that these thoughts create helps us communicate to others that we need their support and kindness. When we are treated unfairly and get angry, our thoughts can help motivate us to take action, make changes in our lives, and change the world. Casually pushing these negative emotions aside without seriously considering their origins can have negative consequences. So, when you focus on the negative, ask yourself, is this negative emotion resulting in action thathas the potential to improve your life? If so, then keep it. If not, then work on changing it.

7. ***Practice gratitude:*** I'll be the first to admit that there is an infinite number of things to be angry, sad, or anxious about. But the truth is that there is also an infinite number of things to feel passionate, joyful, and excited about. It's up to us to decide which we want to focus on.

   One way to train your brain to focus on the positive is to practice gratitude. Gratitude is when we feel or express thankfulness for the people, things, and experiences we have. When we express gratitude at work, we can more easily gain the respect and camaraderie of those we work with. When we are grateful for our partners or friends, they are more generous and kind to us. When we are grateful for the little things in our day-to-day lives, we find more meaning and satisfaction in our lives.

8. ***Savor the good moments:*** Too often we let the good moments pass without truly celebrating them. Maybe your friend gives you a small gift or a colleague

makes you laugh. Do you stop to notice and appreciate these small pleasures that life has to offer? If not, then you could benefit from savoring them.

Savoring just means holding onto the good thoughts and emotions we have. You can savor by holding on to the emotions you're feeling in positive moments. Or you can savor by thinking about positive experiences from long ago. Savoring is a great way to develop a long-lasting stream of positive thoughts and emotions.

9. ***Generate positive emotions by watching fun videos:*** The broaden-and-build theory suggests that experiencing positive emotions builds our psychological, intellectual, and social resources, allowing us to benefit more from our experiences. So, how do we infuse our lives with small bursts of positive emotion?

   One way is to watch positive or fun videos. Watching cat videos or inspirational videos can generate a quick boost of positive emotions that help fuel an upward spiral of positive emotions. Just be sure to mentally hang onto the positive emotions that emerge, through strategies like savoring, so that you take your good mood with you when you leave the couch. And be careful not to get sucked in for too long or you may end up feeling guilty for not getting more done.

10. ***Stop minimizing your successes:*** We have a bad habit of downplaying our successes and not fully

appreciating our wins. For example, we may say, "Anyone could memorize positive words," or "I didn't increase my happiness as much I wanted to." But this fails to recognize the effort that you put in, effort that not everyone would put in. These phrases minimize your small successes instead of celebrating them.

I struggle with this one a lot. People will praise me for building my own business, a business that helps people increase their happiness and well-being. But I'll say, "Anyone could do it. I just got lucky." This kind of thinking downplays all the small efforts I put into make my business successful. Anyone could do it, but they didn't; I did.

The same is true for you. Even reading this post all the way to this point means you are putting effort into improving your ability to think positive. Give yourself some credit for that. As you pursue positive thinking, happiness, or well-being, whatever your goal is, take note of your wins. After every small win, celebrate a little bit.

11. ***Stop all-or-nothing thinking:*** All-or-nothing thinking is when we view a situation as all good or all bad. This is another negative thinking habit that we find tough to overcome. For example, I might think I'm a failure because I have not been particularly successful at helping kids cultivate the skills that help them think positive and increase happiness. I even had to shut down my first business, which aimed to cultivate well-being in kids.

On the other hand, I have had great success in working with businesses to help them develop their happiness apps, writing content for these products and courses, and selling workbooks to help people learn happiness skills. What do you think? Does this make me a failure or success? If I was prone to all-or-nothing thinking, then I'd have to choose one or the other.

There is always room for improvement, but be careful not to start thinking you're a complete failure just because you're not a complete success in all the ways you hoped to be. You win some, you lose some. That's life.

How to Turn Off Negative Thoughts in Your Mind

Barring psychological illness, we are all largely responsible for our own emotional health and well-being. What does that mean? That what we say to ourselves over and over for days, weeks, months, and sometimes years, has a dramatic effect on how we see ourselves. This also contributes to many of the mental health disorders we see rampant today: what we choose to have continually playing in our brains stays there, and there's a real problem when we start buying into the negative thoughts we have about ourselves.

I discovered how powerful the effect of conditioning is firsthand when I was listening to some oldies the other day on the radio. I was amazed at how quickly I could belt out the words to songs I hadn't heard in decades. How could I remember all those lyrics from so long ago? Because I was conditioned by them. I listened and sang those words day in and day out for what seemed like forever, until they were burned into my brain cells, and some of those old songs even provoked strong feelings in me as I took a quick trip down memory lane.

The mind is a powerful thing, and in a nanosecond, it can elevate or crush our mood because of the beliefs lurking behind our feelings. If you think I'm kidding, try it yourself: think of an old song, or even the lyrics to one of your favorite television shows. Those of us who are old enough can belt out the opening line to The Beverly Hillbillies in our sleep.

So, what does all this have to do with our emotional health? Everything. Many of us have problems with negative thoughts playing on the channel of our minds, but if you engage in such thoughts consistently and you believe them, they could erode your sense of self-esteem. Here are a few beliefs that indicate you may need to switch the station:

- I'm a loser

- I'm not good enough

- I don't deserve….

- No one likes me

- I suck at relationships

- I'm a failure

Negative thoughts conjure up bad feelings and hook you into believing that what those old tapes in your head are playing is actually true. In short, they divert your focus to your failures, and that gets you nowhere.

What can you do?

Here are some suggestions:

✓ ***Focus on what you can do NOW, not the past!*** Self-talk is so subtle that we often don't notice its effect on our mood and belief systems. As previously noted, one song can conjure up an entire series of thoughts and memories. Key things to notice are "if only" or "what if" statements: the former keep you stuck in the past with regret, while the latter keep you fearful of the future. There is nothing you can do about the past, and the future isn't here yet, so stay in the present moment.

✓ ***Visualize things on the positive side:*** Three scoops of ice cream: chocolate, vanilla, strawberry. Fresh crushed pineapple and strawberries, warm luscious hot fudge. Ripe sweet banana. Fresh whipped cream and a juicy red cherry. Get the drift? By now, you're not only thinking of the banana split, you can taste it. If we want to change the negative tapes playing in our heads, we have to visualize ourselves positively, which means seeing ourselves non-judgmentally. Picture accepting yourself. How would that look? Draw a picture in your mind and expand on it.

✓ ***Build positive thoughts. Positive actions will then follow:*** Whatever you believe, you'll experience more of, and you'll also find yourself behaving in ways that are congruent with your beliefs. So, start believing the best about yourself: act as if you believe that you're a valuable and worthy person.

✓ ***Recognize and set boundaries to the triggers of negative thoughts:*** Triggers are anything that can start the old tapes playing. If a certain person is a trigger for you, set boundaries with them.

✓ ***Develop positive statements to counter negative thoughts:*** Instead of always putting yourself down in your head, think of some things you actually like about yourself. What are your strengths, what are you good at? Developing counterstatements requires you have some degree of belief in their veracity. Keep your counterstatements in the here- and-now; instead of saying "I'm not good enough", try saying, "I am capable. I'm good at . I accept myself the way I am."

Thinking poorly about ourselves gets us nowhere and is extremely self-limiting. Decide today to turn off the negative self-talk channel in your mind and develop your true potential.

Back at you: If you used to struggle with negative thoughts, how did you overcome this and go on to reach your full potential?

Developing a positive attitude can help you in more ways than you might realize. When you think positive thoughts, you don't allow your mind (be it conscious or subconscious) to entertain any negative thoughts or doubts.

After you learn how to think positive, you will notice

amazing changes all around you. Your brain will actually begin to operate in a state of free-flowing feel-good hormones called endorphins, which will make you feel lighter and happier. You'll also notice a major boost in confidence and will feel more capable of taking on new assignments and challenges that might have previously been outside your comfort zone.

By reducing your self-limiting beliefs, you will effectively release your brakes and experience growth like you never imagined. Essentially, you can change your entire life simply by harnessing the power of positive thinking.

CHAPTER 7

LISTENING TO MUSIC

A growing number of people have discovered how music can help dissolve their daily tension, physical problems such as migraines, and the emotional problems of anxiety and depression. Music and fitness share a common bond in that they both block out or redirect stress hormones, lower blood pressure, ease anxiety, energize and sooth us, and improve our focus. When music and fitness merge, an even stronger bond is formed. We, as fitness and healthcare professionals, have the opportunity to use this music-fitness connection in our aquatic and group exercise classes and personal training and therapy sessions. This makes us all therapists of sorts, and the end result of a class or session is a total mind/body treatment.

The healing power of listening to music is part of the medicinal arsenal that aids us in returning to our fitness activities after an initial illness or injury. Music relaxes us, which causes the release of endorphins (the "feel good" hormones). These endorphins create a way to manage pain and help us return sooner to our fitness activities.

If you want to firm up your body, head to the gym. If you want to exercise your brain, listen to music.

"There are few things that stimulate the brain the way music

does," says one Johns Hopkins, otolaryngologist. "If you want to keep your brain engaged throughout the aging process, listening to or playing music is a great tool. It provides a total brain workout."

Research has shown that listening to music can reduce anxiety, blood pressure and pain, as well as improve sleep quality, mood, mental alertness, and memory.

The Brain-Music Connection

Experts are trying to understand how our brains can hear and play music. A stereo system puts out vibrations that travel through the air and somehow get inside the ear canal. These vibrations tickle the eardrum and are transmitted as an electrical signal that travels through the auditory nerve to the brain stem, where it is reassembled into something we perceive as music.

Johns Hopkins researchers have had dozens of jazz performers and rappers improvise music while lying down inside an fMRI (functional magnetic resonance imaging) machine to watch and see which areas of their brains light up.

"Music is structural, mathematical and architectural. It's based on relationships between one note and the next. You may not be aware of it, but your brain has to do a lot of computing to make sense of it," notes one otolaryngologist.

Everyday Brain Boosts from Listening to Music

The power of music isn't limited to interesting research. Try these methods of bringing more music and brain benefits into your life.

a. ***Jump-start your creativity:*** Listen to what your kids or grandkids listen to, experts suggest. Often we continue to listen to the same songs and genre of music that we used to during our teens and 20s, and we generally avoid hearing anything that's not from that era.

   New music challenges the brain in a way that old music doesn't. It might not feel pleasurable at first, but that unfamiliarity forces the brain to struggle to understand the new sound.

b. ***Recall a memory from long ago:*** Reach for familiar music, especially if it stems from the same time period that you are trying to recall. Listening to the Beatles might bring you back to the first moment you laid eyes on your spouse, for instance.

c. ***Listen to your body:*** Pay attention to how you react to different forms of music, and pick the kind that works for you. What helps one person concentrate might be distracting to someone else, and what helps one person unwind might make another person jumpy.

6 Ways Music Gives Your Brain a Big Boost

Music is one of the few elements that people around the

globe respond in a common way to. It connects all kinds of different people across a myriad of cultures, traditions, and practices all over the world. It's pretty safe to say that music plays a huge role in our daily lives, whether we are aware of it or not.

But exactly how does music really affect one's personality and overall well-being?

The effects of music are cognitive, psychological, social, behavioral, and emotional. Listening to music, singing, playing, composing, and improvising are activities that not only allow one to express inner states and feelings, but also have many positive effects on the people engaged in them. Research shows that music can even make you smarter.

Neuromusicology, a new discipline in science which explores how the human mind reacts to music, is showing that a musical experience involves almost every part and section of the brain at some point. During the musical process, your brain functions more efficiently in many ways. Here are six specific ways music can make you smarter:

1 : Music enhances learning and concentration

According to studies, people who take music lessons regularly develop a better learning capacity than people who do not. Music encourages neuroplasticity, your brain's ability to grow and learn. In the article "Neuroscience of Music – How Music Enhances Learning Through Neuroplasticity", the phenomenon is explained as follows:

"An active engagement with musical sounds not only

enhances neuroplasticity, she said, but also enables the nervous system to provide the stable scaffolding of meaningful patterns so important to learning." "The brain is unable to process all of the available sensory information from second to second, and thus must selectively enhance what is relevant," Kraus said. "Playing an instrument primes the brain to choose what is relevant in a complex process that may involve reading or remembering a score, timing issues and coordination with other musicians."

A musician's brain selectively enhances information-bearing elements in sound. In an integral interrelationship between sensory and cognitive processes, the nervous system makes associations between complex sounds and their meanings. Your brain builds upon these efficient sound-to-meaning connections for other aspects of communication. It enhances the absorption of information, which can help the brain to focus better. Research confirms that music improves some aspects of memory and reading skills.

2 : Music changes the structure and function of the brain

Science has determined that the brains of musicians are structurally and functionally different from those of people who don't play instruments. The size and symmetry of the brain changes. The article "Musicians' brains fire symmetrically when they listen to music" presents the following:

"People who learn to play musical instruments can expect

their brains to change in structure and function. When people are taught to play a piece of piano music, for example, the part of their brains that represents their finger movements gets bigger. Musicians are also better at identifying pitch and speech sounds brain imaging studies suggest that this is because their brains respond more quickly and strongly to sound."

Studies have found that the corpus callosum, the strip of tissue that connects the left and right hemispheres of the brain, is also larger in musicians. This could mean that the two halves of a musician's brain are better at communicating with each other compared with non-musicians. When information transfers more efficiently, memory and other cognitive processes benefit.

3 : Music boosts your overall brain power

As mentioned above, music improves the overall function of the brain. Because of this, it implicitly boosts your brain power. Learning to play a musical instrument is like training for the Olympic Games for your brain. It teaches the brain to problem-solve. There is also some evidence which shows that people who've had musical training are better at math and science.

While the brain benefits are markedly greater for those who start young, it's never too late to reap musical brain rewards. Because your brain remains neuroplastic throughout your life, it can adapt to and improve from learning music at any age.

4 : Music can improve creativity and connectivity

Music improves creativity. Although not all types of music or genres have been shown to have this effect, studies have found that upbeat and happy tunes can encourage creative and innovative thinking. Other research used MRIs to see how the participants' brains reacted to music they especially liked. Those experiments saw that people's brains lit up more in response to their favorite tracks. Scientists discovered that listening to your favorite music makes a huge difference in how your brain responds.

The article "Your Favorite Music Has 1 Major Impact on Your Brain Says Science" quotes the study:

"We speculate that listening to music has the potential to alter brain network connectivity organization and that music preference dictates the connectivity that can be expected," the study authors write. When you listen to music you don't love, the brain's connectivity between memory and emotional centers doesn't light up. In fact, the MRI images hinted that perhaps when listening to music we don't like, our brains are less connected. Based on these findings, it might be possible that listening to preferred music has the potential to engage such brain functions," they write.

5 : Music improves your brain's language skills

People who have language or speaking challenges can benefit from many different therapies, including music therapy. One study discovered that musicians – amateurs and professionals a like – were better able to hear targeted sounds in a noisy environment, which is an important skill for language-learning.

Research using brain-imaging shows that music activates many diverse parts of the brain, including an overlap where the brain processes music and language. This neural overlap suggests that parts of the neural circuitries established for language may have been recycled during evolution for musicality, or vice versa, that musicality served as a springboard for language emergence.

6 : Musical training strengthens the brain's executive function

Your brain's executive functions include numerous critical tasks, from problem-solving and planning to information processing, retaining, and absorption. Musical training has been proven to have positive effects on the executive functions of the brain.

Specifically, one study showed improvement in the areas of cognitive flexibility, working memory, and processing speed, which may explain the link to academic achievement. The brains of children with musical training showed more activation and looked more mature in terms of executive functioning networks. Both children and adults had better executive functioning skills than nonmusicians.

Learning how to play an instrument and to perform songs vocally and instrumentally is a process that requires focused attention and goal-directed behavior. So, the more you train your brain to learn music, the more you ensure that its executive functions are strengthened for other tasks.

Wrapping it all up, the evidence is clear that music causes your brain to function better.

Top 13 Reasons Why Music Works in Our Life

It is a known fact that music relaxes our brain's organization. It raises the level of serotonin, which helps in the spread of nerve impulses and, in turn, aids in the maintenance of joyful feelings. Serotonin also eases tension. When this hormone is limited, a feeling of depression occur. The beat of the music motivates the other beats of the body. Just like the beating of our heart, the effect counters the occurrence of clinical depression.

Music is a joyful activity that affects the whole brain. It is inherent to all of us, humans, and it brings benefits not only for improving memory, focusing attention, or learning languages, but also for bodily coordination and development.

Here is a list of beneficial effects:

1. ***The healing quality of music:*** Listening to music can have positive results on pain management. Listening to it can lessen chronic pains. It can also reduce the sensation and distress of chronic or postoperative pain.

   During childbirth, music is used to decrease the need for medication. It gives a sense of control, and causes the body to release endorphins in order to fight back pain and relax.

2. ***Reduces blood pressure:*** Listening to classical or Celtic songs even for 30 minutes everyday can lower blood pressure.

3. ***Medicine for the Heart:*** The tempo of a good music greatly affects relaxation.

4. ***Speeds up recovery:*** It can accelerate recovery from a stroke.

5. ***It enhances immunity:*** It enhances the immune function. Certain types of music can cause the release of immune-boosting hormones.

6. ***Develops a smart mind:*** According to studies, music can make one learn better because it has the power to develop higher brain function.

7. ***Enhances memory performance:*** It eases the process of recalling information.

8. ***Helps improve concentration and attention:*** Studies show that listening to relaxing music improves concentration.

9. ***Helps body movement and coordination:*** Through music, our muscle tensions are reduced, which leads to an improvement in movement and coordination.

10. ***Music as a fatigue fighter:*** Listening to music can be great when it comes to finding extra energy for the body. It can eliminate the fatigue caused by too much exercise and the exhaustion caused by repetitive and boring tasks.

11. ***Improves productivity:*** Listening to music while working inspires us. Most people work well and perform better in their work while listening to music.

12. ***Relaxes the mind and helps induce sleep:*** One way of overcoming insomnia is by listening to classical music. Studies show that listening to music even for 45 minutes can ensure a relaxing night.

13. ***Helps reduce stress and enhance relaxation:*** Listening to music relaxes not only the mind, but the physical body as well. It helps in the development and relaxation of muscles, which are tensed as a result of long working hours. Music also helps release the tensions caused by a stressful day. When listening to music, especially the upbeat tunes, you will notice that your stresses slowly disappear. As a result, you will become more optimistic and positive.

The Power of Music in a Child's Brain Development

The impact of music on the brain has been a hot topic for parents and scientists in the last ten to fifteen years. More and more studies are proving that children exposed to music have higher IQ's, auditory development, verbal development, and memory skills.

Music is an effective means of triggering and influencing moods, aids in communication, transcends language barriers and encourages interaction with others. The movie, television and marketing industries use music to trigger our emotional response or urge us to buy a product. When we lose someone we love, we listen to sad music; when we are on a long road trip, we tend to listen to peppy music to keep us alert or chase the blues away. If we want to get in the Christmas spirit, we listen to holiday songs.

What Recent Studies Have Found

A Canadian study published on September 2006 in the ScienceDaily, produced evidence that children studying music had improved listening skills and general cognitive functioning related to memory and attention, than those children not studying music. Other studies have found that "assignment to musical training is associated with improvements in IQ in school-aged children." The 2006 Canadian study explored how music training affects the way in which the brain develops. The outcome of the study proved that music is good for your child's cognitive development, and that "music should be part of the pre-school and primary school curriculum."

Northwestern researches have been directly looking into what happens when a child stops taking music instrument lessons after only a few years. What they have found is that adults with one to five years of music lessons had "enhanced brain responses to complex sounds, allowing recognition of sounds in complex and noisy auditory environments." They had more finely tuned auditory perception, decision-making function and auditory communication skills than those with no music training. By contrast, those adults with no music training had less enhanced brain responses. Past studies were focused on the music students who continued their training into adulthood, spending a lifetime in music training. The new study published in the Journal of Neuroscience captures a much larger group, since most children exposed to music training generally do not continue beyond middle or high school.

Exposing your newborn or infant to music and songs benefits them even before they can talk or walk. A McMaster University study discovered that one-year old babies who were exposed to interactive music courses smiled more, connected and communicated better, and showed more sophisticated brain responses to music and songs.

A new study published in BioMed Central's journal, Behavioral and Brain Functions, found that auditory working memory and musical aptitude are "intrinsically related to reading ability," and they found a biological basis for this link via common neural and cognitive mechanisms.

Many parents do not recognize how music affects, influences and benefits their children. It can positively aid in their development and growth from the very start. There are many reasons to expose your child to music, even from within the womb. Here are our top ten reasons:

- ✓ Music aids in brain development, including cognitive, communication, memory and auditory functions.

- ✓ Facilitates the development of self-confidence, self-esteem, self-expression and self- control – all key ingredients to a successful life!

- ✓ Provides emotional well-being.

✓ Stimulates motor skills.

✓ Accelerates language development and improves vocabulary development in toddlers.

✓ Inspires creativity and improvisation.

✓ Motivates concentration.

✓ Encourages interaction with others.

✓ Strengthens the bond between parent and child.

✓ Music is a highly powerful method of setting your child's moods.

There are multiple ways for parents to connect with their little ones and expose them to the great big world of music. The wonderful thing about music is that everyone loves it, and it is so easy to incorporate simple interactive action music games at home or attend an interactive music class. Singing "peek-a-boo my baby girl(boy) or "here is your wiggly little toes" while playing with the babies' feet to the tune of "London Bridge is Falling Down" may seem silly, but the babies will not only find this amusing, they will also learn from it. The rhyming and actions in many silly songs can help your child learn numbers, letters, words and concepts.

Music is a powerful catalyst for learning, creativity, and development. From lullabies to looney tunes and from Bach to Rock, the influence of music and song has a hand in teaching your child. Participate in interactive music and movement classes, play and share music with your child as often as possible! The benefits are a powerful tool for you to help your child grow through the positive power of music.

The Power of Listening to Music

Music which we find enjoyable has an effect on both our emotional and physical states. This may seem fanciful, but is absolutely true. Here are a few of the effects which can be caused by music:

Our brains love to engage in the structure and organization of a good musical piece. This is one reason we feel invigorated after listening to certain music.

Music taps into memories, and playing pieces associated with fond memories brings us joy. Music enhances learning and improves our ability to concentrate and process information.

Music has always been used by humans for social bonding, ceremonies and rituals. It has also been used to convey information. The way in which we respond to music is wired into our DNA somehow, and we can manipulate this to our advantage if we know how.

Rhythm and tempo can cause us to move in response to music. This effect is called "entrainment" and is one of the reasons we dance.

Music can provide extremely effective therapy which is, of course, non-invasive and devoid of harmful side effects.

5 Good Reasons to Listen to Memory-Boosting Music

Now that you know there's scientific evidence for music improving your memory, let's take a look at five wonderful benefits you'll get from this practice. Memory-boosting music will:

1) ***Minimize your stress:*** Stress can cause an unbearable amount of negative thoughts to barrage and cloud your brain. It can also be the reason you feel unmotivated to work or study. Give your brain some rest by using music as a distraction from your stress.

2) ***Improve your mood:*** Listening to happy instrumental music will brighten your heart and mind. Give your ears some nice melodies and don't be afraid to sing along! Singing is a great way to exercise your mind and body.

3) ***Allow you to think more clearly:*** Let your thoughts follow the organized musical patterns and rhythms for you to focus better. Studies show that our brains operate by rhythms. By listening to the rhythms found in memory-boosting songs, you'll be able to study in a clear and calculated manner.

4) ***Keep your eyes on the goal:*** Listening to more alert musical pieces motivates you more and thus enhances your attention. You can essentially be "pumped-up" by a song and use that energy to accomplish the task at hand.

5) ***Allow yourself quick breaks:*** Taking a few moments to hum along with your favorite piece gives you some time to ruminate new information, while also allowing you to reward yourself. The music can be a good reminder that you've been studying too long and need a break.

CHAPTER 8

VISUALIZATION

Visualizing means creating an image of something in your mind. Visualizations have the power to make things more memorable; they stick to your memory better than when hearing something, smelling something or touching something. We do not know why, but it is a fact.

How to

In order to create a visualization, just close your eyes and imagine what you want to visualize. Yes, it is just as easy as it sounds. However, how much effort you will need to put in in order to create the image it depends on how used you are you to visualizing. People have different representational systems, that is, people encode information in their brain using different senses as a base. For those whose main sense is not the visual one, the task of creating visualizations will be more difficult. But do not worry if that is your case; you can build this skill just by practising it.

When you create a visualization in order to memorize something, try to follow the following guidelines:

Include as many senses as possible in the visualization. What are you hearing? How does it smell in there? Can you touch anything? Do not resort to vision only; instead, try to bring all the other senses into play so as to make the visualization as vivid as possible.

Include action in the visualization. Instead of using a simple picture in your mind, observe how the elements of the picture interact with each other. Movies are always better than pictures!

Visualizations should be as appealing as possible. What appeals to you? Sexual or violent images usually appeal to everyone. So, if you incorporate sex or violence into the images created in your mind, this will most likely lead to those particular images being easier to remember.

Visualizations should be as incredible as possible. Make sure to add incredible things to your visualization, like giant monsters or inexistent animals, and make things that are usually inanimate suddenly come to life (like a chair that moves or drives a car).

For example, if you have to memorize a car, then you may visualize a huge vehicle that smells as if it were new, that feels like leather and sounds like an F-1 car. The car has arms and legs which it uses to move along the highway and throw other cars in the air. That's incredible, isn't it? Such an image is bound to stick with you for a very long time!

Now it is your time to practice visualization.

THE WORKOUT

In order to master visualizations, along the next month, perform the following exercises, one each week day. It will only take you 5 minutes per day.

WORKOUT 1: MONDAY

Grab a picture of your choice and observe it for one minute, trying to capture every detail possible. Then close your eyes and try to reproduce the picture in your mind for four minutes. Try to remember as many details as possible.

WORKOUT 2: TUESDAY

Grab an object of your choice (a book, a figure, a plant, etc.). Observe it for one minute, trying to take in all of its details. Then close your eyes and try to reproduce the object in your mind for four minutes.

WORKOUT 3: WEDNESDAY

Observe a room of the place where you are now. Observe it for a minute. Then close your eyes and try to reproduce it in your mind for four minutes.

WORKOUT 4: THURSDAY

Observe the room where you are now for one minute. Then close your eyes and reproduce the room in your mind. Add yourself to the room. Observe how you move around the room and interact with all the things that you encounter there. Use all your senses to interact with the room (smell, touch, sound).

WORKOUT 5: FRIDAY

Observe the room where you are now for one minute. Then close your eyes and reproduce the room in your mind. Add yourself to the room. Move around the room and interact with extraordinary things, like dragons, flying tables, serial killers, martial arts artists that jump very high, etc.

Uses Of Visualizations

Visualizations are used for:

- ✓ ***Meditation:*** Some types of meditation require you to imagine things that directly affect your consciousness and mental state.

- ✓ ***Mood changing:*** You can use visualizations to change your mood, by visualizing a nice situation when stressed, or a powerful result when doubting yourself.

- ✓ ***Goal setting:*** Many techniques applied with the aim of achieving goals imply visualization. It is used to help you set a clear goal in your mind, which you can then work towards.

- ✓ ***Memorizing things:*** Nmemonic systems used for memory improvement have visualizations as their basis. You can use it to remember names, facts, lists of items, telephone numbers, etc.

- ✓ ***Reading fast:*** Speed-reading techniques require that you jump from hearing words to seeing things in order to improve your reading speed. Visualizations are usually required for speeds above 800 Words Per Minute.

Now, if you have understood the rules of visualization, so you are ready to take the next step on the path towards memory improvement.

Describe your plan to your brain in a thousand words, and it will surely get bored mid-way and decide to go to sleep. Draw a picture of your plan in your mind, and it will respond with much deeper interest and attention. While all of this sounds nice and well, though, how can you apply this science to maximize your brain's potential during a 'recession'? Here are some suggestions to get you started:

1. *"...It is now a well-known fact that we stimulate the same brain regions when we visualize something and when we actually do it..."* If, during the recession, you have no idea how to act, start by imagining what you want. What you want will not come immediately, but imagining is a way of getting the process started quickly. For example, if you want to start a home-based baking business, start by imagining being in the kitchen surrounded by cakes and cookies that you are taking out of the oven. Draw a sketch of this, and then draw sketches that come before and after this. The more clearly and repetitively your outline this, the more likely it will be that you will succeed.

2. *"...if a person with this stroke imagines moving the affected arm or leg, brain blood flow to the affected area increases and the surrounding brain tissue is saved..."* If you have had a setback, don't give up. Keep the blood flowing to the brain area that will execute your action by focusing your visualization on what you want. During the recession, people often focus on their fears. All this will do is increase blood flow to the brain regions that

will stop your actions. Remember, a failure is not a final statement that you will not succeed. It is information that your vision has to be changed, refined or repeated

3. *"...visualizations under hypnosis enabled nationally ranked Stanford male gymnasts to execute for the first time se veral complex tricks that they had been working on for over a year..."* Hypnosis here works because it decreases anxiety and increases focus. When you start your visualization, strive to construct the image with your mind free of worries, even if you have to sculpt out an "artificial space" to do this. If you visualize while worrying, it is like painting with a shaky brush. Calmness increases the creativity and authenticity of your "brushstrokes".

4. *"...youth soccer players increased their confidence in play ing when they visualized their moves..."* If you find that the recession has eroded your confidence, use visualization of your goals to help increase your confidence. Practice makes perfect. Repeat these visualizations every day. As you imagine your goal and process more clearly, your confidence will increase enough to execute on your desired goal.

These are a few principles of visualization that can help maximize your brain's capacity as you plan for growth during the recession. Remember, visualization is not just some hokey way of getting to your goals. The principles are grounded in science, and with all the recession chaos going on, it is important to carve out a space where you can use the palette of your mind to paint the pictures that you desire. When you do this, your brain will act in accordance with your visions.

Visualization Creates Changes in Your Brain

Research is constantly finding more and more evidence to support what the ancients have taught for ages, that visualizing or imagining an action creates the same changes in your brain that occur when you actually perform the action. Knowing this gives you amazing power to improve your skills and change your responses to situations. A study was done using PET scans that compared the parts of the brain that lit up when a person performed an action and when that person simply imagined performing the action. The amazing thing is that many of the same parts of the brain lit up in both situations; researchers couldn't really tell from looking at activity in certain areas of the brain whether the person was performing the action or simply thinking about performing it.

If you practice a new skill or activity by visualizing yourself doing it perfectly, you can achieve almost the same amount of improvement as you would if you went out on the court and practiced. This is true for all kinds of sports and other activities, including things like piano, guitar, typing, and so on. You get the idea.

Visualization Can Change Your Brain's Programming

Recent research has also shown that your brain activity undergoes similar changes (observed by using functional magnetic resonance imaging, or fMRI) whether you are remembering an incident in your past, or imagining that incident happening in your future. So, when you sit down to quiet your mind and visualize an activity in your future, or script an event, know that your brain can't really tell the difference between that and your having the actual experience. And why is this important?

Your brain stores data as you move through your life. It keeps track of what you have thought and done, how you did it, and what the results were. And it uses that data to influence your choices of activity and thoughts in the future. If you lean on a hot stove and burn yourself, the next time you come near a hot stove you will most likely remember that burn, and avoid leaning on the stove. And you know how you can smell a fragrance and it takes you almost immediately back to another time in your life? Or you turn into your driveway and you realize that you just drove home without really thinking about it? That is all the result of your brain storing information related to past experiences. The power of visualization or mental practice allows us to feed our brains with new information. And this time, it is information that you want it to have, instead of stuff it has just picked up in daily life. When you understand the power of visualization, you will possess an important key that will allow you to predetermine your reactions and responses to situations in the future and thus be closer to what you desire.

CHAPTER 9

ELIMINATING STRESSORS

On occasion, stress can make certain things memorable. Car accidents, terrorist attacks, and riots can make many things impossible to forget. Such events can even lead to post-traumatic stress disorder.

Usually, though, stress punishes our bodies and minds without the need of catastrophe. Work, relationship problems and health can all create stress. However, stress management may reduce health problems linked to stress, which include cognitive problems and a higher risk for Alzheimer's disease and dementia.

It's not uncommon to feel disorganized and forgetful when you're under a lot of stress. But in the long run, stress may actually change your brain in ways that affect your memory.

Studies in both animals and people show pretty clearly that stress can affect how the brain functions, says Dr. Kerry Ressler, chief scientific officer at McLean Hospital and professor of psychiatry at Harvard Medical School. Scientists have seen changes in how the brain processes information when people experience either real-life stress or stress manufactured in a research setting (for the latter, researchers might challenge subjects to perform a difficult task, such as counting backward from the number 1,073 by

13s, all while being graded). Either type of stress seems to interfere with cognition, attention, and memory, he says.

Stress not only affects memory and many other brain functions, like mood and anxiety, but also causes inflammation, which affects heart health, says Jill Goldstein, a professor of psychiatry and medicine at Harvard Medical School. Thus, stress has been associated with multiple chronic diseases of the brain and heart. In addition, it can affect men and women differently, the professor says.

8 Signs That You're WAY Too Stressed

So, how do you know if you're too stressed?

Chances are you already know when you're stressed. You don't need a checklist to come to that realisation. But just in case, here are some of the symptoms you can watch out for so that you get the chance to improve memory and concentration power starting today.

1. ***Loss of appetite:*** More than just losing the desire to eat, stress can make it impossible to eat. Swallowing even a mouthful can become difficult.

2. ***Overeating:*** On the other hand, stress can make you eat too much. Some people use food as a coping mechanism, something that places even more stress on your system. The heavier you are, the harder your bones and organs have to work. Plus, not feeling positive about how you look is psychologically draining.

3. ***Headaches and Backaches:*** Think that pain in your

head or at the base of your spine is just a part of life? Maybe, but it could also be the symptom of stress.

4. ***Indecision:*** Having a hard time making decisions? It's not necessarily just part of your personality. People who can't define a clear path and follow it could be experiencing too much stress.

5. ***Pessimism:*** It's no wonder that stress makes it hard to see the cup half full. If you're doubtful that your current situation will ever improve, it's not necessarily depression. Stress could be at the core of your dark thinking.

6. ***Obsessing Over the Nuts and Bolts of Life:*** It's good to pay attention to details, but this can also be a symptom of stress. If your perfectionism is getting in the way of your ability to contribute to your family and society at large, you might want to check in with your stress meter.

7. ***Impatience and Irritability:*** Have you suddenly flipped out and chewed someone's head off lately? Such bursts of irritation rarely come from nowhere, so be sure that you aren't acting out based on stress. You probably have other solutions to counteract your struggles other than by getting into conflicts with people.

8. ***Muscle Tension:*** Are your shoulders all bunched up? Do you have pain in your neck? Do you slouch when you walk? If so, you're probably holding stress in your body.

9. And along with muscle tension comes shortness of breath, cramps and even nervous twitching. Even your eyebrows can show signs of muscle tension. Having your face twisted and scrunched up can lead to others thinking that you're grumpy or angry, stressing you out even further.

Horrible, right?

You betcha.

5 Ways Stress Affects Your Brain Power

1. **Chronic Stress Increases the Risk of Mental Illness:** In a study published in Molecular Psychiatry, researchers found that chronic stress results in long-term changes in the brain. These changes, they suggest, might help explain why those who experience chronic stress are also more prone to mood and anxiety disorders later on in life.

    Stress might play a role in the development of mental disorders such as depression and various emotional disorders.

    Researchers from the University of California, Berkeley performed a series of experiments looking at the impact of chronic stress on the brain. They discovered that such stress creates more myelin-producing cells, but fewer neurons than normal.

    The result of this disruption is an excess of myelin in certain areas of the brain, which interferes with the timing and balance of communication. The researchers found that stress can also have negative effects on the brain's hippocampus.

2. **Stress Changes the Brain's Structure:** The results of experiments led by researchers from the University of California, Berkeley revealed that chronic stress can cause long-term changes in the structure and function of the brain.

The brain is made up of neurons and support cells, known as "gray matter", responsible for higher-order thinking such as decision-making and problem-solving. But the brain also contains what is known as "white matter," which is made up of all the axons that connect with other regions of the brain to communicate information. White matter is so named due to the fatty, white sheath known as myelin that surrounds the axons and speeds up the electrical signals used to communicate information throughout the brain.

The overproduction of myelin that the researchers observed due to the presence of chronic stress doesn't just result in a short-term change in the balance between white and gray matter — it can also lead to lasting changes in the brain's structure. Doctors and researchers have previously observed that people suffering from post-traumatic stress disorder also have brain abnormalities, including imbalances in gray and white matter.

Psychologist Daniela Kaufer, the researcher behind these ground-breaking experiments, suggests that not all stress impacts the brain and neural networks in the same way. Good stress, or the type of stress that helps you perform well in the face of a challenge, helps wire the brain in a positive way, leading to stronger networks and greater resilience.

Chronic stress, on the other hand, can lead to an array of problems. "You're creating a brain that's either resilient or very vulnerable to mental disease, based on the patterning of white matter you get early in life," explained Kaufer.

3. **Stress Kills Brain Cells:** In a study conducted by researchers from the Rosalind Franklin University of Medicine and Science, researchers discovered that a single socially-stressing event could kill new neurons in the brain's hippocampus.

    The hippocampus is one of the regions of the brain heavily associated with memory, emotion, and learning. It is also one of the two areas of the brain where neurogenesis, or the formation of new brain cells, occurs throughout life.

    In experiments, the research team placed young rats in a cage with two older rats for a period of 20 minutes. The young rats were then subjected to aggression from the more mature residents of the cage. Later examination of the young rats found that they had cortisol levels up to six times higher than those of the rats that had not experienced a stressful social encounter.

Further examination revealed that while the young rats placed under stress had generated the same number of new neurons as those who had not experienced the stress, there was a marked reduction in the number of nerve cells a week later. While stress does not appear to influence the formation of new neurons, it does impact whether or not those cells survive.

So, stress can kill brain cells, but is there anything that can be done to minimize the damaging impact of stress? "The next step is to understand how stress reduced this survival," explained lead author Daniel Peterson, Ph.D. "We want to determine if anti-depressant medications might be able to keep these vulnerable new neurons alive."

4. **Stress Shrinks the Brain:** Even among otherwise healthy people, stress can lead to shrinkage in areas of the brain associated with the regulation of emotions, metabolism, and memory.

While people often associate negative outcomes to sudden, intense stress created by life-altering events (such as a natural disaster, car accident, or the death of a loved one), researchers actually suggest that it is the everyday stress that we all seem to face that, over time, can contribute to a wide range of mental disorders.

In one study, researchers from Yale University looked at 100 healthy participants who provided information about the stressful events in their lives.

The researchers observed that exposure to stress, even very recent stress, led to smaller gray matter in the prefrontal cortex, a region of the brain linked to such things as self-control and emotions.

Chronic, everyday stress appeared to have little impact on brain volume on its own, but may make people more vulnerable to brain shrinkage when they are faced with intense, traumatic stressors. "The accumulation of stressful life events may make it more challenging for these individuals to deal with future stress, particularly if the next demanding event requires effortful control, emotion regulation, or integrated social processing to overcome it," explained the study's lead author, Emily Ansell.

Different kinds of stress affect the brain in different ways. Recent stressful events (job loss, car accident) affect emotional awareness. Traumatic events (death of a loved one, serious illness) have a greater impact on mood centers.

5. **Stress Hurts Your Memory:** If you've ever tried to remember the details of a stressful event, you are probably aware that sometimes stress can make events difficult to remember. Even relatively minor stress can have an immediate impact on your memory, such as struggling to remember where your car keys are or where you left your briefcase when you are late for work.

One 2012 study found that chronic stress has a negative impact on what is known as 'spatial memory,' or the ability to recall information, the location of objects in the environment, as well as spatial orientation. A 2014 study revealed that high levels of the stress hormone cortisol were connected to short-term memory declines in older rats.

The overall impact of stress on memory hinges on a number of variables, one of which is timing. Numerous studies have demonstrated that when stress occurs immediately before learning, memory can actually be enhanced by aiding in memory consolidation.

On the other hand, stress has been shown to impede memory retrieval. For example, researchers have repeatedly shown that exposure to stress right before a memory retention test leads to decreased performance in both human and animal subjects.

5 Simple Ways To Reduce Stress From Your Life And Improve Your Brain Power

The good news is that solutions exist for each of these stress symptoms. Let's look at some of them.

1. Learn the signs of stress and look for them in your life.

2. ***Train yourself to tune into your emotional state:*** You can best accomplish this awareness through meditation and journaling.

3. ***Seek out an accountability partner:*** An

accountability is someone you contact daily or nearly every day to talk about your commitments, proclaim victory when you've accomplished something and admit your guilt when you've fallen short.

At first, accountability might sound even more stress inducing, but it isn't. Your accountability partner will encourage you and act as a kind of coach. They'll notice when you're pushing too hard, criticizing yourself too much, or when you need to take a break. They will also help you recognize just how well you're doing. You simply cannot have a bad day when you're being held accountable and are committed to holding your partner accountable, too.

It's also freeing to be able to say that you haven't completed something. It's off your chest and you'll hear similar stories from your partner. In other words, you both grow stronger because you report on your efforts to succeed, and together the successes grow, while the failures diminish.

Plus, you help each other see that you never quite fail at all. Every action and every lack of action that you've observed and labeled (which is in itself a form of taking action) lays another brick along the wall of your accomplishment.

I interact with my accountability partner by email because we're thousands of miles apart. But you might be able to meet with yours in person a few times a week. And meeting with people is another way of alleviating stress. These people need to be positive, fun and bring different ideas and perspectives into your life.

Such interactions sharpen your brain, help eliminate stress and create future-minded thinking. Whenever you learn new things, you create a new future that was not possible before. And the more positive the people you hang out with are, the more positive a future you can create.

4. ***Practice breathing and meditate:*** I've talked with you before about pendulum breathing, reverse psychic nostril breathing and progressive muscle relaxation.

   You can practice better breathing while meditating. Meditation is a powerful activity because it improves neural connections, preventing the degeneration of your neurons, and protects your hippocampus. Some scientists believe that the hippocampus is a kind of memory central command centre, but even if not, it's worth protecting this part of your brain in addition to all the rest.

   And meditation is easy to do. You don't need anything fancy. Just your body and a floor to sit on. Contrary to popular belief, you also don't need to try and control your thoughts. As Alan Watts once pointed out, sitting without thoughts amounts to being a stone. Wouldn't you agree that turning yourself into a mindless stone is a useless goal?

   Instead, focus on using breathing and muscle

relaxation exercises to become aware of your body and the flow of your thoughts. Don't try to control your thoughts. As William S. Burroughs once said, "control seeks to control control," which means that you only give your thoughts more power by trying to force them intoshape.

You'll get more from your meditation practice by simply breathing. The distance this creates between your physical awareness and your thoughts will let you realize that the flow of ideas differs little from the beating of your heart. It just happens.

5. ***Chill out:*** Just as you can influence the speed of your heart with exercise, you can exercise the speed of your thoughts. For this reason, I recommend that you wander around your favorite Memory Palace as you meditate and improve concentration Buddha-style.

    You needn't practice recall during these sessions, though you certainly can. The point is to simply give your thoughts a point of focus. In this case, that point of focus is a mentally constructed journey through a familiar location.

    And if your mind wanders to some other line of thinking, no worries. Let it go. Soon you'll become aware of the fact that you're sitting on the floor and realize that you've been lost in thought. These moments of realization will amaze you with their power. It won't be long before you find that similar moments take place throughout the day.

Stress and the Brain

To understand why stress affects thinking and memory, it's important to understand a little about how the brain works. Your brain isn't just a single unit, but a group of different parts that perform different tasks, says Dr. Ressler. Researchers believe that when one part of your brain is engaged, the other parts may not have as much energy to handle their own vital tasks. For example, if you are in a dangerous or emotionally-taxing situation, the amygdala (the part of your brain that governs your survival instincts) may take over, leaving the parts of your brain that help to store memories and perform higher-order tasks with less energy and ability to get their own jobs done. "The basic idea is that the brain is shunting its resources because it's in survival mode, not memory mode," says Dr. Ressler. This is why you might be more forgetful when you are under stress or may even experience memory lapses during traumatic events.

The effect that stress has on the brain and body may also differ depending on when it occurs in the course of someone's life, says Goldstein. Certain hormones, known as gonadal hormones — which are secreted in large amounts during fetal development, puberty and pregnancy, and depleted during menopause — may play a role in how stress affects an individual, says Goldstein. "For example, reductions in the gonadal hormone estradiol during the menopausal transition may change how our brain responds to stress."

CHAPTER 10

HAVE A LAUGH

Laughing is a sure-fire way to release endorphins, and goes a long way in preserving your brain's health. But laughter also opens you up to new thoughts and ideas. That might seem like a big job for something that most of us spend a few minutes doing every day. However, laughter appears to improve the short-term memory of older people. At least that's what researchers conducting a small study at Loma Linda University found.

As part of the study, 20 older adults watched a funny video and were not interrupted or distracted. A control group, on the other hand, sat calmly and didn't watch a video. Afterwards, everyone performed memory tests and had their saliva tested for stress hormones.

Guess who scored best on the memory tests? Yes, those who had watched the funny video. In addition, the researchers noted that levels of the stress hormone named cortisol (gleaned from the salivary tests) were markedly lower as well.

Study author Gurinder S Bains, who is a Ph.D. candidate in Rehabilitation Sciences, had this to say:

"Learning ability and delayed recall become more challenging as we age. Laughing with friends or even watching 20 minutes of humor on TV, as I do daily, helps me cope with my daily stressors."

Humor, the researchers say, lowers your blood pressure, reduces stress hormones and elevates your mood. So, maybe it's time to dropkick that cortisol and have a laugh with your favorite funny movie.

Why Your Brain Loves To Laugh

Who doesn't love a good laugh? We all do, and for good reason. There aren't too many other things that you can do that feel good and are beneficial for you at the same time.

Laughing is not just a fun way to kill time. It has neuropsychological benefits, including improving your mood, exercising your brain, decreasing pain, and strengthening your immune system. It also helps you bond with the people with whom you share a giggle.

What Laughter Looks Like In Your Brain

The physiological study of laughter even has its own name, gelotology. Through experiments mapping the electrical activity of laughing brains, researchers have determined that the production of laughter involves many regions of the brain. Within four-tenths of a second of exposure to something potentially funny, an electrical wave moves through the cerebral cortex, the largest part of the brain. The studies found that if the wave takes a negative charge, laughter results. If it keeps a positive charge, no response is expressed.

The limbic system, an ancient collection of brain structures located deep within the brain primarily involved in emotional and motivational behaviors, seems to be responsible for laughter. Other studies revealed that when brains processed verbal jokes, areas essential to learning and understanding were activated, giving the brain a workout.

A good laugh also causes a chemical reaction that instantly elevates your mood, reduces pain and stress, and boosts your immune system (suppressed by both stress and pain). Research has traced this activity to a region of the brain called the nucleus accumbens, which rewards behaviors such as cocaine use and sex by releasing dopamine, a natural opiate.

"A good laugh can elevate your mood, reduce pain and stress, and boost your immune system".

What's So Funny?

Laughter is triggered when you find something humorous. According to the article "How Laughter Works", there are three traditional theories about what your brain finds funny:

The incongruity theory suggests that humor arises when logic and familiarity are replaced by things that don't normally go together, like when you expect one outcome and another happens. When a joke begins, our minds and bodies are already anticipating what's going to happen and how it's going to end. That anticipation takes the form of logical thought intertwined with emotion, and is influenced by our past experiences and thought processes. When the joke goes in an unexpected direction, our thoughts and emotions suddenly have to switch gears. We now have new emotions, backing up a different line of thought. In other words, we experience two sets of incompatible thoughts and emotions simultaneously. We experience this incongruity between the different parts of the joke as humorous.

The superiority theory comes into play when we laugh at jokes that focus on someone else's mistakes, stupidity or misfortune. We feel superior to this person, experience a certain detachment from the situation and so are able to laugh at it.

The relief theory is the basis for a device movie-makers have been using effectively for a long time. In action films or thrillers, where tension is high, the director uses comic relief at just the right times. He builds up the tension or suspense as much as possible and then breaks it down slightly with a side comment, enabling the viewer to relieve himself of pent-up emotion, just so the movie can build it up again. Similarly, an actual story or situation creates tension within us. As we try to cope with two sets of emotions and thoughts, we need a release, and laughter is our way of cleansing our system of the built-up tension and incongruity. According to Dr. Lisa Rosenberg, humor, especially dark humor, can help workers cope with stressful situations. "The act of producing humor, of making a joke, gives us a mental break and increases our objectivity in the face of overwhelming stress," she says.

The Benefits Of Laughter For Your Brain And Body

1. Laughter releases feel-good endorphins into your system, which actually decrease pain and significantly increase pain thresholds.

2. Laughter can help protect your heart by increasing blood flow and improving the function of blood vessels.

3. Laughter relaxes your whole body for up to 45 minutes after a good laugh.

4. Laughter lowers blood pressure and stress levels.

5. Laughter can increase intimacy and improve relationships.

6. Laughter can reduce anxiety, stress, and depression.

7. Laughter increases the number of T-cells in your body and boosts your immune system.

How To Use Laughter To Improve Your Menatal Health

The use of humor has proven effective in formal therapies for serious mental conditions. Other therapeutic practices incorporating laughter have popped up over the last decade, like laughter yoga. You can include laughter in your daily mental health routine to help ward off depression and stay balanced, or just spontaneously whenever your mood needs a lift. Some ways to do that are:

Keep an eye out for the silly side of life

Try to intentionally notice the silly, unexpected, or funny stuff in your daily life. Savor it, think about it and commit it to memory for when you need a laugh in the future. The most recent time I can remember laughing really hard, I mean tears-rolling-down-my-cheeks-hard, was when my son and I were plunging a stopped up toilet. Who knew those circumstances could be a side splitter?

Reframe unpleasant situations with humor

Try to see the humor in an otherwise unpleasant or embarrassing situation. So, you knocked over your wine glass with an overly demonstrative hand gesture on a first-date dinner (which I totallywould do). Well, at least you made an impression! Or maybe you farted in yoga class. Oops! You're not the first one to ever do that, and isn't it just a little bit funny?

Tickle Yourself

Unfortunately, you can't physically tickle yourself. Research shows that your brain needs tension and surprise for tickling to work, which you obviously don't have when you try to do it yourself. As such, laughter is almost impossible to control consciously. It's very hard to laugh on command, too. You can, however, tickle your own funny bone by watching your favorite funny movies, videos, or television shows.

Laughter makes you feel good. And this positive feeling

remains with you even after the laughter subsides. Humor helps you keep a positive, optimistic outlook through difficult situations, disappointments, and loss.

More than just a respite from sadness and pain, laughter gives you the courage and strength to find new sources of meaning and hope. Even in the most difficult of times, a laugh or even a simple smile can go a long way toward making you feel better. And laughter really is contagious – just hearing laughter primes your brain and readies you to smile and join in the fun.

The Link Between Laughter And Mental Health

Laughter stops distressing emotions. You can't feel anxious, angry, or sad when you're laughing.

Laughter helps you relax and recharge. It reduces stress and increases energy, enabling you to stay focused and accomplish more.

Laughter shifts perspective, allowing you to see situations in a more realistic, less threatening light. A humorous perspective creates psychological distance, which can help you avoid feeling overwhelmed and diffuse conflict.

Laughter draws you closer to others, which can have a profound effect on all aspects of your mental and emotional health.

Other Benefits of Having a Laugh

The health benefits of laughter include the reduction of stress hormones and blood pressure, as well as increased blood flow and oxygenation to the cells and organs. Laughing provides a natural workout for a number of muscle groups, can defend against illness, and even increase the response of beneficial tumor and disease-killing cells throughout the body. Laughter has also been shown to boost memory, intelligence, and creativity.

Nature of Laughter

Laughter is a natural response to stimuli that our individual personalities find funny, whether in the form of images, sounds, physical sensations, or memories.

The physical response of laughter is very fast. After our senses are exposed to something

funny, an electric current runs through our nervous system to our cerebral cortex. The higher brain functions in the left hemisphere decode the words and the syntactical structure in a very analytic approach to the information, while the more creative right hemisphere understands the humor, or 'gets it'. The visual center of our brain then forms an image of the humorous idea, while our emotional (limbic) system releases chemicals that improve mood or promote happiness. Finally, our motor functioning makes us laugh, smile, or double over for a real knee- slapper.

By seeking out humorous situations or participating in activities that will stimulate laughter, you are giving your body a chance to exercise the diaphragm, as well as facial, leg, back, and abdominal muscles. Cortisol and adrenaline levels in the body, which are considered stress hormones, can be reduced through laughter, thereby adding to overall health. Also, the increase in respiration aids in the oxygenation of blood flowing to the brain and the rest of the body.

Additionally, humor is a way to boost the retention of information in academic or professional settings because of the higher number of mental connections between the information and emotional responses (laughter). The number of Gamma-interferon and T-cells, which are the disease and tumor hunters of the body, are increased through regular 'sessions' of laughter, and other sicknesses like respiratory infections and the common cold can be inhibited and decreased if laughter is a regular part of a person's life.

In a very general sense, laughter is a painkiller and reduces the stress and anxiety of physical ailments through the same biological process that is outlined above.

Laughter is also a social mechanism, by which we make friends and connect with others. We often laugh at other people laughing, or at banal statements that are decidedly un-joke-like. The social phenomena of laughter is an important aspect of humor, but its connection to health is not widely studied, and would be better suited for anthropology than health and nutrition.

Health Benefits Of Laughter

Laughter indeed is a medicine for all. Its health benefits include reducing the release of stress hormones, improving one's mood, enhancing creativity and many more.

- ✓ ***Reduces Stress Hormones:*** Laughter has been shown to reduce the levels of certain stress hormones in the body. Although some of these chemicals are necessary for the body in certain situations, high levels without useful application can cause an imbalance in homeostasis and thus have a behavioral impact. These are called immunosuppressant hormones and can have a harmful effect on the immune system. By lessening the presence and production of these stress hormones through "mirthful activity" (like laughing), the overall health and well being of a person can be improved.

- ✓ ***Increases Health-enhancing Hormones:*** On the positive side of hormonal impact, laughter can also increase the number of beneficial hormones, like endorphins, and neurotransmitters in the body. By increasing the level of endorphins in the body, studies have shown that a subject's threshold for pain is increased, making laughter, in a sense, a painkiller or a pain dampener. Endorphins attach to the same receptors in our brain as opiates, making the release of endorphins like a drug experience without the negative side effects, along with easing mood, tension, anger, and pain. An increase in neurotransmitters means that your brain is able to function faster, make connections more rapidly, and comprehend situations and problems at a higher rate.

- ✓ ***Boosts Immune System:*** Laughter can even go so far as to help you stay healthy. It has been widely affirmed that laughter can stimulate antibody cells to develop at faster rates by changing the body's chemistry through hormonal shifts. This increase in antibodies means that the body is able to fight off illness and infection more easily. T-Cells are a type of white blood cells known as lymphocytes. Studies have shown that the efficiency of T-cells is actually increased in a subject who regularly laughs and adds those hormonal advantages to their overall system.

✓ ***Natural Exercise:*** Aside from the internal benefits of laughter, it can also be a natural way to exercise various muscle groups in your body. When you engage in laughter, whether it is a giggle or a guffaw, muscles are used to create that movement. The old adage that it "takes more muscles to frown than to smile" is somewhat true, unless you are laughing while smiling. Laughter engages the body's diaphragm and abdominal muscle systems during that repetitive expanding and contracting that often happens when laughing for an extended period of time. This is why our sides or stomach hurt slightly after long bouts of laughter.

The facial muscles are also exercised, the same as they would be when singing or enunciating strongly. Depending on your laughing style, and how physically engaged you become, you can work out your legs, back, shoulders, and arm muscles as well.

✓ ***Complementary Cancer Therapy:*** While studies are needed to show the direct positive impact of laughter in cancer treatment, Dr. William B. Strean,

University of Alberta, found that a number of cancer survivors have used humor as a complementary therapy. Since laughter is linked to improving natural killer cell activity, it can help increase disease resistance and decrease morbidity in those with cancer or other chronic diseases (Alternative Therapies in Health & Medicine 2003).

✓ ***Regulates Blood Pressure:*** For anyone with high blood pressure, try to laugh more and watch your blood pressure decrease. Studies have shown that "mirthful laughter" causes an initial increase in arterial blood pressure due to the physical act of laughing, but that rise is followed by a decrease to below the normal resting blood pressure. This is further proof that laughter does indeed improve circulation and can reduce blood pressure, which is one of the major causes of heart disease and cardiac issues for many people.

✓ ***Increases Blood Oxygenation:*** The process of laughter causes us to use our respiratory system very quickly and strenuously for a short amount of time. This intense activity stimulates an increase in the blood flow as the heart rate increases temporarily, thus increasing the amount of oxygen flowing to the brain. Increased oxygen levels in the brain promote healthier brain function, as oxygen is integral to brain health. Additionally, the pulmonary activity gets a boost from laughter as well, because there is a higher level of ventilation of the lungs during robust episodes of "mirthful laughter".

✓ ***Improves Memory:*** Along with the improved brain function that laughter can provide, it can also work to improve memory in a different way. The connections and associations that the brain forms while "learning" can be widened and made more complex by combining basic learning with an emotional response like laughter or humor. Varying the levels of association with different parts of our brain (pleasure, amusement, logic, reason, etc.), remembering facts and recalling details is easier because there are more linkages present in our memory.

✓ ***Enhances Mood:*** Studies have shown that the simple act of laughing or smiling can improve the mood and happiness levels in subjects versus other activities. Laughter has been found to have analgesic properties, which means that it reduces even unconscious pain, causing an improvement in mood. Even forced laughter, without a normally humorous stimulus, works to improve mood. Therefore, even if you don't have anything funny to laugh about, simply participating in the physical of laughter will probably put you in a better mood. Your brain does not actually register whether the stimulus is genuine or not, since people often find unusual things funny or laugh at inappropriate times. Research suggests that good mood may lead to a greater preference for healthy foods overindulgent foods.

✓ ***Promotes Creativity:*** Laughter has a large number of effects on the chemical processes in the body, and the combination of reduced stress hormones, increased endorphins, and increased oxygenation to the blood and brain causes an increase in creativity in test subjects who laugh often. By improving overall brain health and bolstering its natural support system, both hemispheres can work together more efficiently, so creativity has a place to foster and grow.

Why Laughter Is So Good For Your Brain?

All of us are guilty of this one thing. We have all watched a funny video and laughed out loud in the office at least once in our lives. Well, you need not feel too guilty about it. Laughter is great for your brain, and the more chances you get to have a genuine laugh, the better your overall health is going to be. "Laughter is the best medicine" is not just a popular saying; it has ample scientific backing, too. After all, laughter has multiple health benefits – for example improving immunity and the cardiovascular system – but its effects on the brain are truly amazing.

March 19 is celebrated as National Let's Laugh Day in the USA, and it's right around the corner. On this occasion, let's look at all the amazing ways laughter improves our lives, and more specifically, our brains.

Anatomy of laughter

Laughing is considered one of the most natural and instinctive expressions available to humans. But what goes on behind the skull during a laugh is not even remotely simple. Laughter, in fact, uses a sizable chunk of the brain by connecting and working out several areas of it at once.

Let's break down the progress of laughing that takes place in your brain following humour researcher Peter Derk's experiment:

Analysis of words or situations happens in the left side of the cerebral cortex.

The large frontal lobe and the limbic system beneath the cortex (that processes nuanced emotions) get activated.

The right side of the cortex works out the distinct trigger of laughter, or to say in lay terms, "gets" the joke.

Brainwaves are sent out to sensory processing areas located in the occipital lobe.

The areas responsible for motor functions are activated to produce the physical act of laughter.

CHAPTER 11

SMART DRUGS

S mart drugs are special brain supplements that work on targeted neurons and neurotransmitters to improve various aspects of brain functioning such as focus, attention, memory, wakefulness, mental alertness, and learning ability. Unlike other brain supplements, these drugs naturally work on the neurons and brain cells, and help improve the short term and long term memory of a person in different ways.

A great thing about smart drugs is that they cause little to no side effects during and after use, and the positive effects are clearly experienced by the user in most cases. People use different smart drugs for different purposes, ranging from studying to anxiety to wakefulness.

For example, there is a smart drug called Noopept, which is 800-1000 times more potent (by weight) than the oldest racetam and gives more benefits for less dosage than any other smart drug available on the market today.

How Smart Drugs Help Boost Brain Power

Smart drugs work in different ways to boost the brain and give optimum benefits to their users. However, the effects vary from person to person depending on a range of factors, such as their age, gender, and health. In multiple studies conducted on smart drugs, it was observed that:

They improve the production of endogenous chemicals called neurotransmitters, which are responsible for proper communication between targeted neurons.

They stimulate the production of hormones such as dopamine and serotonin, which control energy, focus, mood, and a number of other mental activities.

Smart drugs help delay the aging of brain cells and promote the growth of existing brain cells.

They also act as natural stimulants for the brain and help the user perform well in a range of memory-related activities.

Smart Drugs and Nootropics

There is a common myth among users that the terms "smart drugs" and "nootropics" are interchangeable. Even Wikipedia says so. Just search for the term "smart drugs" on Wikipedia and you'll be redirected to a "Nootropics" page. To be clear, nootropics are a type of smart drug, but not all smart drugs qualify as nootropics.

What is the difference between Smart Drugs and Nootropics

Smart drugs are sold as prescribed medication and are mostly consumed for their off-label use – mostly to treat cognitive disorders and improve the mental functioning of the user. Good examples of smart drugs include Adderall and Ritalin, drugs that are used to treat ADHD symptoms, and

Modafinil, a popular productivity booster.

On the other hand, nootropics are not necessarily prescribed by doctors; many of them are available over the counter. They can be synthetic, like Noopept, or made of herbs, vitamins, antioxidants, and a range of chemical ingredients that deliver a natural positive impact on the brain and ultimately improve brain power in multiple ways. In a nutshell, nootropics belong to the family of smart drugs and are used for specific purposes by users.

Smart Drugs for Brain Power

Rigorous analysis finds that the drug modafinil significantly enhances cognition during complex tasks.

What if you could pop a pill that made you smarter? It sounds like a Hollywood movie plot, but a new systematic review suggests that the decades-long search for a safe and effective "smart drug" might have notched its first success. Researchers have found that modafinil boosts higher-order cognitive function without causing serious side effects. Modafinil, which has been prescribed in the U.S. since 1998 to treat sleep-related conditions such as narcolepsy and sleep apnea, heightens alertness much as caffeine does.

A number of studies have suggested that it could provide other cognitive benefits, but the results were uneven. To clear up the confusion, researchers at the University of Oxford analyzed 24 studies published between 1990 and 2014 that specifically looked at how modafinil affects cognition. In their review, which was published in 2015 in European Neuropsychopharmacology, they found that the methods used to evaluate modafinil strongly affected the outcomes. Research that looked at the drug's effects on the performance of simple tasks such as pressing a particular button after seeing a certain color did not detect many benefits.

Yet studies that asked participants to do complex and difficult tasks after taking modafinil or a placebo found that those who took the drug were more accurate, which suggests that it may affect "higher cognitive functions, mainly executive functions, but also attention and learning," explains study co-author Ruairidh Battleday, now a medical doctor and Ph.D. student at the University of California, Berkeley.

Don't run to the pharmacy just yet, though. Even if many doctors very likely prescribe the drug off-label to help people concentrate better, a 2018 study found that 22 percent of Americans had

taken prescription brain-boosting drugs in the past year and that 4.1 percent had used modafinil. Trials have not yet been carried out on modafinil's long-term effectiveness or safety. Studies of the drug have been "carried out in a controlled scientific environment and usually only looked at the effects of a single dose," explains neuropsychologist and review co-author Anna-Katharine Brem, then at Oxford, so no one yet knows whether it is safe for long-term use in healthy people. Nor is it known whether modafinil might lose its edge with repeated use, a phenomenon familiar to many coffee drinkers.

Side effects are another important consideration. Modafinil has been shown to cause insomnia, headache and stomachache in select users, and some research suggests it could be addictive. Although these kinds of problems may be worth enduring for a drug that treats an illness, "if you don't have a medical condition, the risks versus benefits change dramatically," says Sharon Morein-Zamir, a psychologist at the University of Cambridge who studies ethical considerations associated with the use of cognition-enhancing drugs. "For some, the benefits will likely outweigh risks, at least some of the time," she says, whereas "for others this may not be the case." A pill you take to ace an exam, for instance, won't do you much good if it also causes a grueling stomachache.

Should Everyone Take Cognition-Enhancing Drugs?

As is the case with all medications, cognition-enhancing drugs affect different people in various ways. Setting aside the ethical questions about brain boosters, here is a look at groups who may deserve special consideration.

1. ***Children and Teens:*** Cognition-enhancing drugs could present unique risks to the developing brain. Several clinical trials found modafinil to be safe when given to children with attention-deficit/hyperactivity disorder (ADHD), but the trials lasted only a few months, making it difficult to ascertain the potential effects of long-term use. In a 2014 review article examining the biochemical effects of modafinil and other common "smart

drugs," researchers at the University of Delaware and Drexel University raised concerns that the use of these drugs could affect the developing brain's ability to adapt to new situations and might increase the risk for addictive behaviors.

2. ***People With Lower IQs:*** Research suggests that cognition-enhancing drugs offer the greatest performance boost among individuals with low-to-average intelligence. These findings led University of Oxford researchers to propose in a 2014 paper that if such drugs were selectively given to people who need them most, many ethical concerns about the drugs' use would be alleviated, and they might even reduce opportunity inequality.

3. ***Seniors:*** Some studies suggest that older adults may not derive much benefit from cognition-enhancing drugs. One study found that methylphenidate (Ritalin), which boosts working memory and attention in young adults, had no effect on performance among healthy elderly volunteers who were asked to perform various cognitive tasks.

The Search For An Intelligence Drug

People have been searching for ways to boost their brainpower perhaps for all of history. In the past century, scientific efforts have revealed a few promising chemicals, but only modafinil has passed rigorous tests of cognitive enhancement.

1. ***CAFFEINE:*** One of the oldest and most popular

stimulants. People recognized the stimulant properties of caffeine hundreds (perhaps thousands) of years ago. It can enhance alertness and attention; however, its effects are short-lived, and tolerance builds up quickly.

2. ***NICOTINE:*** Also a stimulant, used for hundreds of years for a range of medicinal purposes. It is very addictive and has many dangerous side effects.

3. ***AMPHETAMINE (BENZEDRINE, ADDERALL):*** First synthesized in 1887. Benzedrine was the first drug to treat hyperactivity in children. Amphetamine can enhance attention and memory by increasing levels of norepinephrine and dopamine in the brain, but the compound can be addictive and comes with a range of side effects, including hyperactivity, loss of appetite, disturbed sleep, even psychosis.

4. ***METHYLPHENIDATE (RITALIN):*** First marketed in 1954 and prescribed in the 1960s for treating hyperactivity. It became popular for ADHD in the 1990s. As with amphetamine, it can improve memory and focus for those with ADHD, but it is also used off-label as a study and work aid. Some individuals build up a tolerance to Ritalin over time.

5. ***ACETYLCHOLINESTERASE INHIBITOR (ARICEPT):*** Approved to treat Alzheimer's disease in the 1990s. In some studies it has been shown to enhance memory and attention in healthy individuals.

6. ***MODAFINIL:*** Originally used to treat narcolepsy. It can also enhance cognitive function, especially when completing difficult tasks. Experts are not quite sure how it works or what long-term effects would look like.

CONCLUSION

Everyone wants a better and smarter brain to process information faster and have better memory recall. The truth is that the most brilliant minds don't have more brain power than the average person, they just use their brains more efficiently.

Your brain's health is a product of your daily habits.

To optimize your brain, all you have to do is make slight adjustments to your routine.

10 days offer just enough time to realistically adopt new habits that can help you get smarter and think better, yet long enough to be challenging.

In 10 days or less, you can adopt some of these habits to boost your brain power, improve your mental clarity and build a better brain.

Start mindfocus exercises.

Embrace meditation.

There's plenty of research that shows meditation increases the grey matter in your brain.

Meditation can increase the thickness of regions that control attention and process sensory signals from the outside world.

Yes, meditation makes your brain bigger (literally). Meditation is the art of silencing the mind.

When the mind is silent, concentration is increased and we experience inner peace. But concentration requires a great amount of effort and time.

In less time than it takes you to have lunch, you could be expanding your brain. Quite literally.

Just like building muscles, you can beneficially build the strength and even the size of your brain in the healthiest and most natural of ways.

Meditation has been proven to benefit the brain.

"Although the practice of meditation is associated with a sense of peacefulness and physical relaxation, practitioners have long claimed that meditation also provides cognitive and psychological benefits that persist throughout the day," says study senior author Sara Lazar of the MGH Psychiatric Neuroimaging Research Program and a Harvard Medical School instructor in psychology.

The problem is getting started.

It's kind of like going to the gym. We all know we should do it, but put it off all the time. If you do decide to give meditation a try, though, you can use Headspace, an app that bills itself as "a gym membership for your mind."

- ✓ Stop feeding your comfort.
- ✓ Comfort provides a state of mental security.

- ✓ When you're comfortable and life is good, your brain can release chemicals like dopamine and serotonin, which lead to happy feelings.

- ✓ But in the long run, comfort is bad for your brain.

Without mental stimulation, dendrites, connections between brain neurons that keep information flowing, shrink or disappear altogether.

An active life increases dendrite networks and also boosts the brain's regenerating capacity, known as plasticity.

"Neglect of intense learning leads plasticity systems to waste away," says Norman Doidge in his book, "The Brain That Changes Itself".

Michael Merzenich, a pioneer of plasticity research, and author of "Soft-wired: How the New Science of Brain Plasticity Can Change Your Life" says that going beyond the familiar is essential to brain health.

"It's the willingness to leave the comfort zone that is the key to keeping the brain new," he says.

Seeking new experiences, learning new skills, and opening the door to new ideas inspires us and educates us in a way that improves mental clarity.

Anything that makes you really comfortable is not really good for your brain

When you are inside your comfort zone you may be outside of the enhancement zone.

"Your brain needs novelty to grow," says Jones. Stepping out of your comfort zone literally stretches your brain by allowing the dendrites to become like big trees with full branches rather than little shrubs.

- ✓ Your brain needs you to read every day.

- ✓ Reading heightens brain connectivity

- ✓ Our brains change and develop in some fascinating ways when we read.

As you read these words, your brain is decoding a series of abstract symbols and synthesizing the results into complex ideas.

It's an amazing process.

The reading brain can be likened to the real-time collaborative effort of a symphony orchestra, with various parts of the brain working together like sections of instruments to maximize our ability to decode the written text in front of us.

Reading rewires parts of your brain. In her book "Proust and the Squid: The Story and Science of the Reading Brain", Maryanne Wolf explains:

"Human beings invented reading only a few thousand years ago. And with this invention, we rearranged the very organization of our brain, which in turn expanded the ways we were able to think, which altered the intellectual evolution of our species… Our ancestors' invention could come about only because of the human brain's extraordinary ability to make new connections among its existing structures, a process made possible by the brain's ability to be reshaped by experience."

Reading involves several brain functions, including visual and auditory processes, phonemic awareness, fluency, comprehension, and more.

The same neurological regions of the brain are stimulated by reading about something as by experiencing it.

According to the ongoing research at Haskins Laboratories for the Science of the Spoken and Written Word, reading, unlike watching or listening to media, gives the brain more time to stop, think, process, and imagine the narrative in front of us.

Reading every day can slow down late-life cognitive decline and keeps the brain healthier.

- ✓ Exhaust your brain.

- ✓ Challenge yourself with a whole new experience.

- ✓ Do more of what exhausts your brain.

- ✓ Your brain needs exhaustion to grow.

Take up new, cognitively demanding activities — something new you've never done before: dancing, piano lessons, a foreign language — is more likely to boost brain processing speed, strengthen synapses, and expand or create functional networks.

"When you're learning something new and your brain is feeling like it wants to take a nap, that's when you know you're doing things that are growing your brain neurologically, not just maintaining it," says Dr. Jennifer

Jones, a psychologist and expert in the science of success.

Every time you learn something, you create new connections, and the more connections you can maintain, the easier it will be to retain new information in the future.

Start a journaling habit

Getting a full night of sleep, going for a run, maintaining a healthy diet, and keeping up with family and friends all have well-documented and significant impacts on overall cognitive function.

What's even more important for your total well-being is journaling.

Journaling helps you prioritize, clarify thinking, and accomplish your most important tasks over urgent busy work.

Numerous studies (of the scientifically rigorous variety) have shown that personal writing can help people better cope with stressful events, relieve anxiety, and boost immune cell activity.

Judy Willis MD, a neurologist, and former classroom teacher explains, "The practice of writing can enhance the brain's intake, processing, retaining, and retrieving of information, […] it promotes the brain's attentive focus, […] boosts long-term memory, illuminates patterns, gives the brain time for reflection, and when well-guided, is a source of conceptual development and stimulus of the brain's highest cognition."

✓ Don't sit still.

- ✓ Sitting still all day, every day is dangerous.

- ✓ Love it or hate it, physical activity can have potent effects on your brain and mood.

The brain is often described as being "like a muscle". It therefore needs to be exercised for better performance.

Research shows that moving your body can improve your cognitive function. What you do with your body impinges on your mental faculties.

Find something you enjoy, then get up and do it. And most importantly, make it a habit. Build a better exercise routine and maintain it.

Simple aerobic exercise such as going for a 30 to 45-minute-long session of brisk walking, three times a week, can help fend off the mental wear and tear, and improve episodic memory and executive-control functions by about 20 percent, according to Art Kramer of the University of Illinois at Urbana- Champaign.

Take a good and undisturbed sleep

A good sleep reduces both physical and mental stress.

The brain accomplishes the reorganization of information during sleep.

Importantly, a short afternoon nap (called the power nap) serves as an energy booster for the brain.

Scientists have known for decades that the brain requires sleep to consolidate learning and memory.

Far from being lazy, napping is scientifically proven to help improve concentration and boost productivity when you reach a brain power plateau.

Studies on napping suggest that it increases reaction speed and helps with learning — provided naps are no longer than 20 minutes.

Do nothing for a change!

Doing nothing is a skill.

Busyness can be counterproductive.

It's hard, we know, but doing nothing is a good way to refocus your brain and help you pay attention to the present time.

Spending time unplugged, disconnected, and in silence can improve your focus, productivity, and creativity.

"Learning to do nothing will help you retake control of your attention at other times, too. One trick: schedule 'do nothing' time like you'd schedule tasks. Just don't expect others to understand when you decline some social event on the grounds that you're busy not being busy," says Oliver Burkeman.

Neuroscience also reveals that silence has nourishing benefits for your brain.

The neuroscientist Marcus Raichle says his best thinking happens in quiet places. For Raichle, silence was shorthand for thoughtful solitude.

The brain is actively internalizing and evaluating information during silence.

Improve Your Memory And Get More Brain Power

When it comes to the well-being of our brain, memory plays a vital role. Without it, our mind would not be able to perform most of the simple tasks that seem so common to us. For our brain's sake, it is essential that we find ways to improve memory as soon as possible.

Without having our memory functioning properly, we could get into some serious problems. For example, when crossing the street, a tragic accident would happen if we forgot to check if there are any vehicles coming. What if, when cooking, we forget about our activity and leave the house unattended? Just imagine the major upsets a poor memory can cause you. A good memory is priceless and we have to do everything we can to keep it that way.

Sometimes, our own memory can play tricks on us, and we have to recognize those moments, analyze them and determine the factors that cause them. Many times our memory is not necessarily responsible for our inability to recall information. Often times, our overall health is the one causing problems.

For instance, when we are stressed out, our brain is weak, and as a consequence we can't entirely concentrate on our present actions. Our brain is mainly focused on the 'pain' factor and leaves very little energy for other mundane chores. According to memory specialists, multitasking is not good for memory. That's why our mind needs to focus on one thing at a time in order to obtain optimal results.

There are moments when we simply don't pay enough attention to the things in front of us. We are distracted by our surroundings or our emotions and we lose focus. In such cases, our memory can't recall things that were not memorized in the first place. It has been established that if you want to transfer anything to your long-term memory, you need to focus on it for about 8 seconds.

There are prescription drugs which can be used to improve our brain's memory but we have to be aware of the various side effects that might occur. And if we are on other types of medication, we need to know if they are compatible with our memory prescription drugs. Before taking any medication, you need to consult your doctor.

Not only humans rely heavily on the proper functioning of their memory. Animals need it as much as we do. In some cases, their memory is just about as complex as ours. Think about all the animals that perform at a circus show. They are trained to remember and execute to perfection all kinds of complex exercises.

All that seems amazing to us, but who knows what kind of pain they had to go through until they finally understood what the trainers want from them. In some cases, humans rely on the animals' ability to recognize certain things. Police dogs are trained to find hidden drugs, some animals are used as guides for blind persons and so on.

Many things are taken for granted and we realize how

precious they are only when we lose them. Memory is one of our brain's most precious treasures and thus needs to be well-maintained and cherished.

www.ingramcontent.com/pod-product-compliance
Lightning Source LLC
Chambersburg PA
CBHW061349250726
48657CB00004B/1402